Geron and Virtus

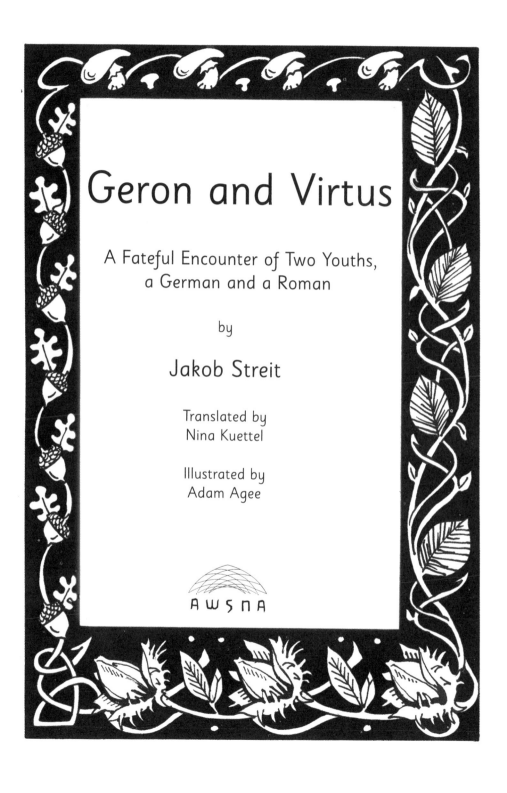

Geron and Virtus

A Fateful Encounter of Two Youths,
a German and a Roman

by

Jakob Streit

Translated by
Nina Kuettel

Illustrated by
Adam Agee

A W S ∩ A

Printed with support from the Waldorf Curriculum Fund

Published by:

**The Association of Waldorf Schools
of North America Publications
3911 Bannister Road
Fair Oaks, CA 95628**

Title: *Geron and Virtus*
Author: Jakob Streit
Translator: Nina Kuettel
Editor: David Mitchell
Proofreader: Ann Erwin
Cover design: Hallie Wootan
Illustrations and cover art: Adam Agee
© 2006 by AWSNA
ISBN # 1-888365-70-6

Table of Contents

The Raid

At a castle not far from the Rhine River, three young Roman cavalry soldiers were starting out on a day's ride. They had been given a three-day pass to go hunting. Up to now they had hoped to get a bear, but, so far, they had only three rabbits. Now they were sitting lazily around the campfire over which Livius, the oldest, was roasting one of the rabbits. They were enjoying the aroma of the roasting meat with great anticipation. Close by, their horses were nibbling on leaves from the trees to which their reins were tied. Livius said: "Tomorrow we'll ride deeper into the German forest. If we go back without a bearskin we'll be the laughingstock of our comrades!"

Octavian, a somewhat chubby and more jovial boy, answered him: "We've already gone a little too far north into no-man's-land. At present our enemy, the Germans, don't dare come any closer to our castle. A few of the yellow-haired ones have already been captured. In the city of Castra Vetera they pay a good price for them as slaves. We would get more money for a young German lad than for a bearskin. Why don't we go on a hunt for Germans? What do you think, Virtus?"

Now the youngest, a youth with a slim but still strong build, offered his opinion: "I'd rather go on a bear hunt than a manhunt. I've wanted to have a good hunting adventure for a long time now! My father warned against going too far into the German forest. It's probably better if we go back."

During this conversation the three youths did not notice that their campfire was being observed from a short distance. A German boy, smelling the smoke from their campfire and hiding behind the thick bushes, had crawled fairly close. He was curious to see who had built a fire, and he had tied his horse to a tree further below. His clothing, made from animal skins, was good camouflage. Now he was observing the soldiers and also stealing glances at the beautiful Roman horses. He wanted to get back right away to his hunting companions to tell them the news about the Romans.

His companions were camped a little deeper in the same forest. There were five of them, all experienced hunters. They were breaking off pieces of deer meat to satisfy their hunger and drinking barley water from leather canteens. A lively discussion was in progress about their enemy, the Romans. One of them raised his voice: "Not far from here, in the Teutoburg Forest, together with our commander, Armin, we gave those Roman wolves a beating. They came to destroy the sacred things of our ancestors and make slaves of us. Very few Roman soldiers under Varus's command escaped from that forest battle. After the battle was lost, Varus fell upon his own sword! Here, look at this dagger. I took it off of a fallen Roman soldier. That was twenty years ago, but it is still a good hunting knife. And over there you see my spear. It's also Roman."

Wugo, an old hunter, was the one who had spoken. Gerold also had something to add to the conversation: "The Romans have become more bold of late. We can't fish anymore in the Rhine River. They're everywhere with their soldier boats. Since they built all those stone military forts on our side of the river, we have to be very careful that they don't swallow up all of Germania. The Roman wolf is greedy!"

Wugo replied: "The German bear is strong. Back then in the Teutoburg Forest, the Roman wolf ran off with his tail between his legs."

While the men were talking their young companion rode swiftly into camp. He was gasping from excitement as he sprang from his horse: "Not a half hour from here are three Roman soldiers. They're cooking a rabbit on the spit, have splendid horses, and are well armed." For a moment the surprise was complete. Then voices were raised all at once, each talking over the other: "Let's take them! Man and horse! Shield and sword!"

The half-gnawed bones were thrown away and the fire put out. The young rider took the lead. For the first little distance they rode, but then they tied their horses to some trees on the edge of the forest meadow. The hunters stole noiselessly through the trees. Soon they caught the faint odor of smoke. Inch by inch they drew closer. The Romans had no clue as to what was happening. They enjoyed the rest of the rabbit and were laughing and making jokes. They drank some Roman wine. The hunters were deciding in quiet whispers which two of them would attack which Roman and bind him fast.

At the signal, the hunters broke out of the underbrush with terrifying screams. Two of the Roman soldiers remained seated on the ground, paralyzed with fear. The oldest jumped up. He drew his short sword in order to defend himself. But at that moment he was hit with a spear and fell to the ground. If the horses had not been tied securely, they would have been long gone. As it was, the Germans went merrily on their way with their Roman spoils.

At Hamarson's Smithy

Hamarson the blacksmith was standing at the anvil in his rock cave hammering a piece of iron. His helper walked in and called out to him: "Hamarson, there's a big group of men riding up here!" The blacksmith put down his hammer and curiously looked out of the cave. Sure enough, the men were headed toward the smithy which was next to his log house. A greeting of "Hali!" echoed up, and Hamarson returned it with his own baritone "Halo!" But three of the horses had no riders. Two of them were being led by two Roman soldiers with their hands tied together. The horses' reins were tied to the soldiers' belts. The third Roman horse was coupled with another horse. Evidently, his rider had been lost.

Hamarson jovially greeted the hunters who were all well-known to him. He was happy for them and their fortunate adventure. Old Wugo said: "We've come to an agreement about the spoils. For my part, I'm taking this boy as my slave. My two old farmhands could use some younger help. Hamarson, do you have any extra leg irons I could put on him so he doesn't escape from me?"

"Yes," answered the blacksmith, "I have two pair available. I worked on them last winter."

Wugo was a little tight-fisted. When he heard that the going rate for leg irons was an entire steer, he became sour and said: "Two sheep would have done just as well!"

Hamarson laughed in his face and said: "Iron is expensive and the art of blacksmithing is hard work!" So, Wugo somewhat unwillingly gave him his handshake. He had a raw manner and he took out his anger on the young slave Virtus by hitting him with his fist and yelling: "Get inside to the blacksmith!" The young man got suddenly pale, then the blood rushed to his face. As a noble, free Roman citizen he had never been struck with a fist. On top of that, he did not understand one word of the German language. However, it was suddenly clear to him that he was not only a prisoner but a slave as well and must be blindly obedient.

Hamarson frowned when he saw Wugo's behavior and thought: "Poor boy, you're getting a foul master." He took Virtus by the arm in an almost friendly manner and led him into the smithy. The other prisoner was also brought inside. Hamarson took the leg irons down from a hook on the wall. The wide leg irons were fitted above the ankle and tightened with such big pliers that they could never be taken off unless it was done by a blacksmith.

Wugo ordered his slave to jump up on the horse and ride behind him. In chains the slave would not have been able to keep up with a horse. Hamarson helped him up on the horse. All the other hunters said their goodbyes to Wugo and rode with their slave and the rest of the spoils to the North. But Wugo rode in an easterly direction. As he was saying goodbye, he assured Hamarson: "In the next few days I'll send one of my old farmhands to you with the steer."

The Old House

The sun rose on a clear, late summer day. It peeked over a hill in the forest and shone onto an ancient house. It was covered with thatch and looked as if it was half sunken into the ground. In places on the roof where the thatch was rotten, moss and grass were growing. Instead of a front door, as we know them today, there was a bearskin hanging over the opening. A gray-brown dog was lying in front of the low door and appeared to be asleep. Suddenly the dog raised its head, listened for a moment, and jumped to its feet. He started wagging his tail and prancing around on his paws as if in great anticipation. He had noticed that someone was nearing the door.

The bearskin was pushed aside. A strong, large youth appeared, dressed in short, furry pants made from some kind of animal skin and a sleeveless linen shirt. As he held up his bare arm to run his hand through his blond hair, the dog jumped on him, joyously barking. The boy grabbed him by his front paws, went three or four steps with him and rolled him on the ground. Then he ran away lightning fast with the dog barking after him. The boy grabbed a piece of floating wood from the nearby stream and gave it a hefty toss into the distance. The dog chased after it like the wind. The boy went into the water up to his knees. He splashed water into his face and hair. Then he shook his hair like a horse shakes its mane so that drops of water sprayed out on all sides. He was just putting his arms in the water again when the dog reappeared and lay the stick on the ground at the edge of the stream. The boy said: "Good dog, Waldo." Then he went to him and patted his fur.

A quick grab, a throw, and with a powerful arc through the air, the stick landed in the crown of a tree. The dog went wild when he saw the stick hanging from a branch. He tried in vain to get it down. Geron, the boy, continued washing his muscular arms. He drank water from his cupped hands. Waldo sprang at him again and with his barking gave Geron to understand that he must get that stick back. Geron glanced upward, walked to the tree, and swung himself effortlessly from branch to branch. The dog silently watched what would happen next. His master let the stick fall through the branches.

Geron made himself comfortable up there in the branches and looked over at the old hut. The bearskin was pushed aside. Gerda, his little sister, came outside. She looked all around, rushed to the stream, but could not discover where her brother was. She called out in a high voice: "Geeeeroooon!" But her only answer was the call of a cuckoo bird from somewhere in the distance. She did not notice that it was a "human" cuckoo. Gerda called once again, this time noticeably louder and a little agitated: "Geroon!"

"Cuckoo, cuckoo!" The sound was definitely coming from the linden tree.

"Aha," thought Gerda. "The cuckoo bird has blond feathers. I'll go and get him!" With light feet she sprang across the meadow to the linden tree and called up: "Come down here! The cooking fire is gone out and Mother says you have to light it again!"

There was a noisy, rustling sound. Geron slid through the branches and landed next to Gerda on all fours. Fast as a weasel, she jumped onto his back and wrapped her legs around his waist. She popped him on the shoulder and cried: "If you can be a cuckoo, you can also be a horse!" Her good-natured brother stood upright and trotted off. She grabbed his hair like the reins and pulled him to the left and right, here and there, and woe to him if he did not obey! Gerda was a very energetic little girl.

Mother was sitting by the fireplace and greeted him: "The fire stones are blind today. I am having no success. Would you make the fire spirits dance?!" She put two gray stones in his hands.

Geron examined them and said: "One of them is moist from sweaty hands. That's why it won't spark." He rubbed the stone for a little while on a piece of sheepskin and asked: "Mother, where did Father go with Gerwin?"

"Early this morning, while you were still asleep, they rode to Holding to borrow a second ax from him. Father took him the rabbit he killed yesterday in exchange for it. He allowed Gerwin to ride your horse. Your brother must also learn how to ride. I think they should be back soon. That is why I must get the fire going. Father can become angry when there are no coals in the fire. I don't know how it came to go out in the first place. I believe the wood that Gerwin brought me yesterday must have been wet."

Geron had been practicing making fires for years, and he had become pretty good at it. Still, there were days when even he could not get a fire started. He took some of the old ashes and rubbed them between his palms in order to cleanse his hands for the fire making and dry them out completely. Then he struck the fire stones against each other and directed the sparks toward a little pile of fine, dried grass.

Gerda walked in, but she knew that one was not to be disturbed during fire making. She quietly knelt next to her big brother in anticipation of the new fire. Softly, she began to sing the song that her grandmother, Uralda, had taught her:

> Sparkling spark, flaming fire!
> Fiery sparkle, glowing coal!
> Sparkling spark, flaming fire!
> Fiery sparkle, glowing coal!

Grandmother Uralda came hobbling out of the darker recesses of the hut. When she saw both of her grandchildren looking so contented in the firelight, a smile further creased her already wrinkled face. She sat down beside them on a wooden stool and let herself be enveloped by the warmth of the fire. Gerda asked: "Grandmother Uralda, who gave mankind fire and taught them to get it from the fire stones?"

Uralda searched in her pockets and brought forth a few oat kernels. She said: "In ancient times the gods gave fire to mankind. We must give thanks for every new fire! Geron, take these three oat kernels and throw them one after the other into the fire. After each time I will say one of the three names that consecrates the fire. That way, it will do us no harm."

Geron threw the first kernel into the fire. Uralda said: "Lohe, blaze forth!" With the second kernel: "Lodher, give warmth!" With the third kernel: "Loge, give light!" And with every name Uralda bowed her head and made a sign with her hand toward the fire that looked like a zig-zag of lightning. Geron knew that it was the holy symbol of the god Tyr. Once again he took some of the old ashes and slowly rubbed them between his palms and let them fall into the flames. That is what unites the old fire with the new.

Mother came in with a leather pot. She had fetched water from the stream. She praised Geron: "My, you did that fast! I thank you!"

Outside, Waldo began to bark. The sound of horses hooves could be heard. Father and Gerwin were home. Gerda was the first one out the door. Mother and Uralda were right behind her. Geron rubbed the rest of the ashes off his hands with some dried grass and threw it in the fire. By the time he got outside his father had already dismounted from his horse and was showing his wife and Uralda the borrowed ax. He said: "Look, how wide it is! It's a Roman ax. Holding traded it for a bearskin."

Gerda wanted to climb up with Gerwin on the horse. She called: "I want to go for a ride with you! Stay on the horse! I can't do it alone yet!"

Gerwin, her twelve-year-old brother, was only too happy to take his little sister for a ride. He looked over at his father and asked: "Can the little quaky frog go a round with me?" Gerwin loved to give his sister animal nicknames.

Father replied: "The horses have to carry a lot of wood yet today. Another time."

Geron, who had just now come outside, added: "Gerda has ridden enough for one morning. She whipped me around the meadow for all I was worth!" He laughed, grabbed his sister, pulled her from behind Gerwin on the horse, and said: "Down from there!"

Gerda held onto Gerwin who was holding onto the horse's mane so he would not fall off. But Gerda tickled him until he could stand it no longer. With a cry of frustration, he let himself fall to the ground. The horse was frightened because of the noise and ran away with Gerda, the dog Waldo barking after them. Gerda held fast to the horse's mane and tried to keep her balance. Uralda threw up her arms in alarm.

Geron put his fingers between his teeth and his lips and let out a loud whistle. After all, it was his horse and it knew his voice and his whistle. Rappen, the horse, was almost to the stream. The whistle brought him to a stop. He looked around with a wondering gaze, walked to the edge of the water, and wanted to drink.

Gerda slid off his back and gave the runaway a friendly pat on his neck. After that he willingly let the girl lead him back. Gerda was a little worried. What would Father say?

When she reached the hut, Mother said severely: "You might have broken your arm or a leg!"

Gerwin teased: "There's no 'quaky' left in the little frog! Too bad she didn't get plumped down in the water." Gerda looked at her father. He said nothing, but she could not see any anger in his eyes and his mustache seemed to be hiding a smile.

Geron took the reins from Gerda and said shortly: "Not bad, Gerda." Oh, that was like a soothing balm for her after the terrifying ride.

Uralda put her arm around Gerda and whispered: "I said a magic word for you. It helped. You didn't fall off the horse."

The New Log House

Father German put the Roman ax that he had acquired from Holding into Geron's hands and said: "Now we can go into the forest and fell some trees. The ax is freshly sharpened. Each one of us will chop until we're tired and then the other will take it up again. Gerwin can use our smaller ax to chop the branches off the fallen pine trees. Holding is coming this afternoon with his son, Holger, to help us. Then we will chop the logs and fit them together at the building site. The new house must grow fast, or the winter will be here before it has a roof."

Gerda quickly interrupted: "Is Helga coming too?"

Father replied: "No, she is helping her mother. You can take the sheep from their pen down to the pasture now. But take Waldo with you and a good stick. Holding told me there's a Wolf prowling around the forest. He loves to eat sheep. Be sure to stay with them!"

After the workload had been divided up, Father said: "Gerwin, take both axes and go ahead of us to the place in the forest that has been prepared. Geron and I will come shortly after we've put the collar on the horse and readied the pulling ropes."

On the way to the forest Gerwin came upon the site for their new house. He walked over there and examined how high the logs were that had been laid down one on top of the other. They were already taller than he was. The door opening was already covered by a log, and Gerwin walked through it to what would be the inside of the house. He was so happy about the new house. Even Father would be able to walk through the door without stooping. It would be much roomier than the old house.

Gerwin hit a few stumps with the back side of the ax and listened to the dampened tone they gave off similar to a voice. Uralda had told him: "Something from the tree spirit that was driven out when the tree was cut down is still echoing in the trunk."

Gerwin suddenly felt a little creepy, being so alone in the new house. He hurried on to the forest. While he was waiting for Father and Geron he could try out the Roman ax on a felled tree trunk and chop away a few branch buds to make the log smooth. Soon the chips were flying. The borrowed ax was really sharp! Father and Geron arrived with the horse. Now Gerwin had to use the small ax and chop three times for every one time that was needed with the Roman ax.

German went a little to one side to a high pine tree. Like other trees around the clearing, this one also had the two ax marks indicating it was to be cut down. Gerwin let his ax rest for a little while and watched how his father walked up to the tree and wrapped his arms around the trunk. He pressed his forehead into the bark and mumbled some words that Gerwin could not make out. Geron had also put both his hands on the pine. He knew that Father was asking the spirit of the tree to move into another younger tree because he had to cut this one down. And, also, he asked that the tree spirit would not be angry with him. Three times he knocked the trunk with the dull side of the ax and waited a while.

Then Father made a powerful chop with the ax. After some time had passed Geron took over. He was almost as powerful as Father, and in a short time the ax had eaten away at the tree trunk. Geron gave the ax back to his father. The last blows were the most important and the most difficult. One had to be careful that the tree fell in the desired direction.

Suddenly Gerwin heard a loud gnashing and ripping noise. He thought: "The tree spirit is fleeing!" The pine fell to the ground with a loud, cracking noise.

Father went to fetch the thin tree trunk that served as a measuring device for the length they needed. He said: "The top part of the trunk where it is thinner will be put aside as a rafter for the roof." Geron began separating it with the ax. Gerwin started chopping off branches. He worked so diligently that he had to stop often to catch his breath.

German used the horse and the rope to pull the tree trunk that was prepared yesterday to the building site. When he returned he saw that the new trunk was already divided and almost free of branches. He praised both of the boys for their good work.

Gerwin took the opportunity to ask: "Right, Father, when the house is finished you'll give me a real knife, since I'm working so hard?!"

Father replied: "We'll see if I can find one. Maybe Hamarson the blacksmith would trade one for a sheep."

Just then they heard someone calling hello. Mother had come with food and drink. Gerwin let the ax fall and said: "Good that you came. I hadn't even noticed that I'm practically dying of thirst!" He grabbed the water jug out of her hand and slurped the water like a young calf.

Mother put down a big wooden bowl containing barley gruel and divided up the wooden spoons. All four sat down and held their spoons over the food while Father spoke a few words of thanks, as was the custom. Gerwin asked: "May I put something good into the barley?"

Geron teased: "Have you gathered wood chips?"

"No, I took some seeds out the pine cones. If you eat them you'll grow big. That's what Uralda told me."

Father laughed and said: "Just put them on your spoon. You need them the most!"

Suddenly they heard someone calling. Gerwin quickly stood up: "They're coming! Holger and Holding! I've eaten enough!" And off he ran. He had stuck his spoon into the barley and thrown the pine kernels into the bowl. Holding, a man of powerful build, was leading a plow horse. Holger was sitting atop the horse. A little older than Gerwin, Holger was a slim boy with clever eyes and white-blond hair.

Everyone gave a short but hearty greeting. German praised the Roman ax. Holding showed them their older broad ax: "Here, I brought our old one along. With this ax we can easily get the logs to fit together. There are some iron chisels in the leather bag." Holding was an experienced house builder and very well-known in the area for his talent. He was often asked to help build a new house for weeks at a time. He promised German he would help for three days.

"This is going to be great," said Gerwin to Holger. "You spend the night with us tonight and tell us stories about gnomes, giants, and monsters. I'll ask your father if it's all right for you to stay here tonight. He will probably want to ride home."

In a short time pine tree after pine tree came crashing down. German and Holding took turns using the Roman ax. After each of them had used it twice, the tree would fall. Towards evening more logs could be taken by the horses to the building site. Geron and Holger took care of that job. After they had taken the last log over to the house site, they freed the horses from their collars and let them graze. The two young men sat down on a log for a little rest.

Holger admired Geron. He was strong and good at everything he did. Holger had wanted to become good friends with Geron for a long time, but it was difficult when they saw each other so seldom.

Holger reported: "Three days ago I went with Father to visit the old hunter Wugo and his wife Runege. She's a strange woman. It seems like she's always trying to practice some kind of magic. I don't know where he got him, but Wugo turned up with a young Roman slave. Wugo makes him milk the cows and such. Hamarson the blacksmith put him in leg irons. The slave always has to carry the chain when he walks. It is a terrible hindrance to milking, chopping wood, and working in the fields. Wugo says that the Romans also do that with the German slaves they capture."

"How old is he and what does he look like?" Geron wanted to know.

"About a year older than you. He's strong. He has black hair and dark eyes. Even though he's a Roman, I still feel sorry for him. Wugo didn't want me to talk to him. He speaks very little German and has a German symbol branded on his arm."

Geron said: "Let's go visit him sometime in secret, maybe when he's working in the field. Do you want to? I've been curious to learn more about the Romans for a long time. They make such excellent axes!"

Suddenly Holger whispered: "Look there on the edge of the forest. Is that a wolf?!"

Geron jumped up: "He's sneaking in the direction of the sheep pasture where Gerda is!" Before Holger knew what was happening Geron had grabbed a thick stick, ran to his father's grazing horse, swung himself on the horse's back, and galloped away toward the sheep pasture. Holger mounted his plow horse as well, but that horse could not be forced to break a walk.

The wolf was making his way to the grazing sheep flock. Gerda was dozing in the shade of a tree. Waldo was asleep at her feet. There was a loud noise! The sheep scattered in all directions, bleating and terrified. The wolf had caught a lamb. Half carrying it and half dragging it, he headed toward the nearby forest.

Waldo ran after the wolf to try to take the lamb away. At that moment Geron rode into the pasture. Since the wolf was paying attention to the barking dog behind him, he did not notice the horse bearing down on him from the front. Geron grabbed onto the horse's neck with his left hand and took the stick in his right hand. He gave a hefty blow to the wolf's head. The lamb fell, bleeding, into the grass. Geron used the moment to spring from his horse and deal the wolf a death blow.

Waldo was barking and bearing his teeth, but he did not make a move without Geron's permission. The wolf shuttered slightly and then lay still. He was dead. The poor lamb was struggling without a sound in the grass. The wolf had bitten it in the neck. It could not be saved, so Geron quickly put it out of its misery. By this time Holger had arrived on his workhorse. He saw Geron standing between the wolf and the lamb, trying to catch his breath.

The sheep were still scattered. Geron waved to his sister for her to come closer. She slowly walked forward, the shepherd staff held high for defense. When she saw that the wolf was dead she let the staff fall. Without greeting Holger, she went to the dead lamb and knelt beside it. Her tears fell upon the little lamb's soft wool. She felt a hand stroking her hair. When she looked up she saw Holger's sad eyes. He spoke softly: "The lamb's soul is going up, over the the white, woolly clouds. He's leaving his wool here for you. He is giving you a nice, warm winter hat." And Gerda saw that after Holger spoke these words his eyes were no longer sad.

Geron came up and said: "Holger, put the lamb on the horse. I will take the wolf home. It has to be skinned quickly." He lifted the lamb onto Holger's horse.

Gerda remembered: "I have to gather the sheep. Come, Waldo!"

Before Holger got on his horse, he bent down, picked a flower, and handed it to Gerda with these words: "Look, a tiny drop of blood from the lamb is on the petal. Take it with you and thank the gods that Geron's arm was strong enough to kill the wolf!"

Holger swung himself up on to the horse, holding the lamb in front of him. He slowly rode toward German's house. Geron took the wolf and, with a powerful heave, laid it crosswise on his horse's back.

Most of the sheep had run wildly back to the old hut and sought shelter in the bushes. Mother Ina and Uralda both realized at the same time that something bad must have happened. They both started out in the direction of the sheep pasture to see about Gerda. Halfway there they came upon the two boys, Geron and Holger. Geron quickly explained what had happened. Ina hurried on ahead to help Gerda look for some of the sheep who may have strayed.

Uralda turned around and limped back home. She murmured to herself: "I've never had a sheepskin and a wolf skin on the same day. Not a bad sign, I would say." Soon she had taken up a knife and was hard at work. The boys rode back to the building site, very late, picked up the horse collars and returned to the forest where they had been chopping trees.

Uralda was working on the lamb skin. She very carefully cut it away from the flesh. The meat was cut into chunks. While she was working she kept saying soft words for the dear little lamb. A little while later Ina and Gerda returned with the stray sheep. They helped Uralda to skin the wolf. The meat was put into a wooden container and the fat into a special bowl. Gerda had to get cooled wood ash from the fire inside with a small wooden shovel. Then she was to sprinkle the ash over the pieces of wolf meat. Uralda explained: "The good ashes cleanse the wolf blood. Now it cannot harm us."

Back in the forest the two fathers were upset that their boys were taking so long to return when there was so much work to be done. When Geron and Holger finally did return, they were unpleasantly surprised to see the angry looks that awaited them. But Geron defused their anger when he called out loudly: "The wolf is dead! Gerda is all right!"

But sometimes anger is not as quick to leave as it is in coming. Father German's voice was harsh when he ordered: "Tell us what happened!"

Gerwin hurried up to the group. He was nervously chewing on his pine kernels. Geron reported the events. When he was finished Holding came up to him and gave him a big hug. He exclaimed: "You were magnificent! From now on I will call you the wolf killer. And when the house is finished I will put the wolf's skull under the rafters as a reminder of your brave act. It will also keep bad spirits away."

German's eyes were blazing with pride. All the anger had disappeared. He said: "You may come along on the next bear hunt, Geron. Tonight you shall put the wolf's head on top of a high anthill. The ants will clean it until nothing is left but the white bones. We will make one more trip with the logs today and then it's quitting time. There's a wolf at home that needs butchering and for dinner there will be lamb. You will stay and eat with us, won't you Holding?"

Holding answered: "I'm always ready for roast lamb. And tonight we must celebrate our wolf killer. If you have enough room, Holger and I will stay the night with you, since the animals are outside now. My wife already said we should probably stay here. A little roast wolf also wouldn't be bad, if it's not such an old one that your teeth get worn down with the chewing!"

The Lamb and Wolf Roast

All the women in German's house were hard at work preparing a feast for the men. Gerda explained: "I won't eat one bite of wolf meat, and my little lamb . . . I just couldn't eat it!"

Her mother said: "Then you can eat some sheep cheese." Gerda was happy with that and began to carefully cut up the herbs that Uralda needed for the meat. Ina had already prepared a large, hot-burning fire. There were two spits with meat on them, one for the lamb and the other for the wolf. In one pot wolf soup was simmering.

Uralda took an old sword from the wall and used it to cut up large pieces of meat into smaller ones. Gerda was amazed at how forcefully she could cut the bones with the sword.

Uralda picked up a single piece of meat, stuck it onto the tip of the sword, and lay it in a special place on the coals. Gerda asked: "What is that piece of meat?"

Uralda answered a little gruffly: "That is the wolf's heart. Geron must eat it. Give me some ground herbs, the chamomile and the 'balderbrau' so that I can sprinkle some on the meat."

Gerda brought her grandmother the herbs she asked for and questioned: "Why the balderbrau? Isn't that the herb of the sun god, Baldur?"

Uralda answered: "Because it improves the wolf meat and gives the heart strength when Geron eats of it. For this reason we always sprinkle some on all the wolf meat, not just the heart."

Outside, Waldo's barking told them that the woodsmen were returning. Geron had hardly entered the house when he asked: "Where is the wolf's head?"

His mother answered: "I cut it away from the pelt. It is hanging here over the door. Otherwise, Waldo would have gotten it for sure." Geron took it down. Gerwin held up a burning rush lantern for light. Men and boys alike gave it a close examination.

"Middle-aged," estimated Holding. "Should still be edible! Ha, ha! But right now, boys, you must take it to an anthill. The fresher it is, the happier the ants are to gnaw on it." The three boys went to the edge of the nearby forest to where Geron knew there was a large anthill. He carried the wolf's head by the ears. Uralda had not cut out the tongue. She said: "Those who eat wolf's tongue become liars and slanderers!"

When they reached the anthill it was pretty dark. The ants were already underground. Geron laid the head on top and pressed it back and forth. The disturbance caused the ants to become agitated. Gerwin stuck his face very close so as to observe close up how the ants dug into the bounty. But he stuck his nose a little too far forward, lost his balance, and fell face forward into the anthill simmering with ants. In no time they had crawled onto his arms, legs, inside his shirt and pants. He screamed and ran away. But the biting and stinging had only just begun.

Gerwin did a wild dance on the meadow, writhed in the grass, tore off his shirt and pants, slapped his arms and legs, shook himself like a wet dog, and screamed again. Geron and Holger could contain themselves no longer. They both started laughing uncontrollably. Gerwin swam around in the grass a few more times and then slowly regained his composure and lay motionless on his stomach.

Holger gathered up the pants and shirt. He carried them in two fingers, shaking them out all the way to the house. He called to Gerwin: "I'm going to leave them in the smoke for a little while and then I'll bring them back to you!"

Geron walked up to his brother and encouraged him by saying: "Stand up and I'll help brush off the ants!" But Gerwin continued lying there and grumbled: "I'm staying outside. I'm not hungry." Geron understood that Gerwin wanted to be left alone. He went back to the house.

Inside, Holger had already told the story about the ants and the clothes and everyone was chuckling. Only Ina said: "Poor Gerwin!" Holder held the clothes close to the fire. Two or three ants fell out of them. Uralda fetched some freshly picked fern leaves, gave them to Holger and said: "Take some of the sheep fat and rub it in with these leaves before he puts his clothes back on." Ina knew that Gerwin would be well looked after by Holger.

A warm evening wind was blowing when Holger went back outside with the clothes and the ointment. The moon was shining over the late summer meadow. Gerwin was still lying on the ground. His skin felt like it was on fire. Holger said softly: "Uralda gave me some herbs and sheep fat for your skin. It will take away the pain." He rubbed a few leaves between his hands and let them fall onto Gerwin's skin. Then he rubbed the fat onto Gerwin's burning skin. Gerwin happily let him continue. He showed him the places that were especially painful.

Slowly Holger used up all the fat and Gerwin was already feeling better. He put his clothes back on. Holger took his hands and said: "Gerwin, please forgive me for laughing so hard. It's just that you looked so funny. We didn't mean to make fun of you. I'm sorry. If you are unable to sleep tonight, I will tell you a long story. I'll whisper it to you so we won't awaken the others."

That meant a lot to Gerwin. He nodded and thought how wonderful it was that Holger was helping him. Holger put his arm on Gerwin's shoulder as they walked back to the house and said: "Listen, Gerwin, when we get back to the house, the others will laugh and have some fun with you. Don't let it bother you. Laugh with them! One has to learn to go along with the teasing sometimes." Gerwin was amazed at Holger. He seemed so much wiser and yet he was only about a year older than Gerwin.

When they arrived at the house the others had already started the wolf soup. Everyone was cheerful. Holding laughed loudly: "There comes our little ant dancer. I'll bet your meat was tastier to them than that old wolf's head!"

Holger gave Gerwin a little nudge from behind. Gerwin said: "Dancing makes me hungry. Do I also get some of that soup?" Ina handed them both wooden spoons. They sat down in the circle and the conversation continued.

German said: "When my grandfather became old he had a hard time walking. The Druid priest told him to lay with his naked back against an anthill as long as he could stand it and then do it again a week later. He did it and was able to stand it a good long while. The first thing that happened was that he got a high fever. But, after that, walking was much easier for him. After the second time on the anthill, all the pain disappeared from his legs and he could walk as good as new. See, Gerwin, since the ants got to you as a boy, you'll have strong legs your whole life."

Holding laughed again in his own jolly, loud way. He added: "Hey, now, where is that wolf roast?"

German and Geron lifted the roasting meat from the spit. But before anyone could dig in, Uralda said: "Stop! First, Geron gets the heart!" She took the sword out of the coals and lay the roasted meat onto a piece of tree bark. She put it before Geron, gave him a curtsy, and put the meat into his hands.

Holding called out in his powerful, bass voice: "Good luck and good health to the wolf destroyer!" And everyone chimed in with their agreement.

Ina gave each of the men a piece of the meat, and soon everyone was enjoying the feast. Gerda nibbled on bread and sheep cheese. Ina passed around the drinking mug containing cool milk. Everyone was so busy chewing that at times one heard only the crackling of the fire. From time to time Mother put another stick of wood on the fire for better light. Holding remarked: "Look there, the Wolf Destroyer has eaten the heart. Soon he will be growling and howling like a wolf himself."

And sure enough, Geron started to growl and howl very loudly just like a wolf until Waldo let out a big bark from outside. Geron got down on all fours and snapped the bit of meat out of Holding's hand. Holding loved fun and games. He was laughing so hard that everyone else started laughing as well, even Gerwin.

When everyone had had their fill of wolf meat, German brought the lamb meat from the coals. Gerda disappeared in the straw in order to go to sleep. Conversation lagged and when someone did say something it was in a soft voice. Holding said: "I understand why wolves go after lambs. It's food fit for the gods!" Uralda was able to join in the feast when the lamb was served but her nearly toothless gums could not handle the tough meat of the wolf.

Everyone was full so Uralda stood and went over to the fire. She threw a bit of the lamb's wool and some hairs from the wolf onto the coals. She thanked the fire spirits who had so splendidly roasted the meat:

> Flicker, flicker, crackling coal,
> Flaming spirits glowing,
> Roasted meat has filled our bowl,
> Our gratitude we're showing.

With those words she threw a few pine needles onto the burning coals. A sweet smelling perfume permeated the little hut. The talking gradually ceased and the fatigue from a full day's work began to make itself felt. Everyone said: "Goodnight" and lay down in the straw. Geron had gathered the leftover bones onto a tree bark platter. He brought them to Waldo outside. Waldo stood guard over the house at night.

Holger's Bedtime Story

Gerwin was lying in the straw trying not to notice the burning, stinging sensation over his entire body. Every so often he would shiver. He had a fever. Actually, the pain had become more bearable but he could not even think about sleeping. Holger, who was lying next to him, whispered: "Gerwin, are you not able to sleep? Would you like to hear a story now?"

Gerwin answered: "Yes, Holger, please tell it!"

One could already hear the deep, regular breathing of the others who had fallen asleep as Holger quietly began to tell his story:

Once upon a time there was a shepherd boy who took care of the sheep. When evening came he sought out a place to rest next to a pine tree. There were many rocks lying about, both large and small. Suddenly the shepherd boy thought he heard the delicate voice of a gnome. It was saying: 'Please free me! Please free me!' The boy noticed that the voice seemed to be coming from underneath one of the larger rocks. He dug his staff under the rock and moved it to the side.

A little gnome who had been squashed flat stood up. He shook himself for a while and slowly his normal appearance returned. Now he was looking at the boy. He raised his finger and said: 'I thank you for freeing me. A bad troll squished me under this rock. I would like to grant you a wish. What would you like?'

The shepherd boy thought about it for a moment and said: 'Would you show me the way into the land of the gnomes?'

The gnome looked at him with an expression that could not be described as pleased. The gnome asked: 'Can you remain silent? Because on your first visit to the gnome kingdom you may not speak one word of human language!'

The boy answered: 'Since I'm with the sheep all the time I'm used to not saying anything.'

The little man winked: 'Come on, then.' He trotted in front of the boy and they went into the forest. By a rock formation the gnome pushed two branches aside to reveal the entrance to a cave. The little man put his fingers to his lips to remind the boy that he must remain silent, and they both stepped inside.

The gnome took the boy by the hand. In the darkness it was impossible for the boy to see past his outstretched arm.

But after his eyes had grown more accustomed to the darkness he could see a bluish light shining ahead.

Suddenly there were many little folk jostling around the two visitors. Many of them pointed again and again at the shepherd boy. They were obviously amazed that he was so big. And they also grinned because he had no beard.

They came to an open room in the cave. Laured, King of the Gnomes, was seated upon a crystal throne. The little gnome had to ask the king's permission: 'May this human boy look at the treasures of the mountain? He rescued me from underneath a magic rock where I had been put by a bad troll. He freed me.'

The king answered: 'Bring him closer to me! I want to test him first.' The shepherd boy was very anxious standing in front of Laured while the king examined his face in the light of his crystal.

The boy put up his hands and called out: 'No! No!' Suddenly he heard thunder and everything around him went dark. When he awakened he found himself outside again under the pine tree with his sheep. The little gnome had carried him out. If only he had remained brave nothing bad would have happened. He would have seen many wondrous things in the depths of the earth. After that, the boy would often look behind the bushes where he thought the secret cave entrance to be, but he never found it again.

Holger was silent. Gerwin whispered: "Holger, how can one get courage? I'm often scared as a rabbit. I get afraid in the middle of the night and don't want to go outside. I'm afraid of the gnomes, elves, and bad spirits. Are you able to go outside at night?"

Holger answered: "Yes, I've done it. Often, in the night, when everyone else is asleep, I go outside and wander around the meadow. I have seen some strange things. They're real you know, the gnomes, elves, trolls, and strange spirits. I can see them the best in the moon shine. Then I protect myself with a holy sign that the Druid priest Evart showed me. When I'm old enough I also want to become a Druid."

Gerwin asked him: "Who has the say whether you may or may not become a Druid?"

Holger replied: "Once Father agrees, then I would have to go to the Druids for one week. During the week they examine your courage, perseverance, ability to remain silent, and devotion."

Gerwin thought it over and then said: "How is one's perseverance tested?"

"Well," Holger answered, "that can happen in various ways. For instance, you're stood before a fallen pine tree with ax in hand and told to cut up the entire tree into small shavings, from the thick trunk to the slender top. You begin at sunrise and chop until sunset and if you're not yet finished, then you continue working without light until it's completely dark outside. If you're not finished by then, you must begin again at sunrise until you finish the job. The Druid Evart told me this."

Gerwin thought again for a little while and asked: "How do they test your devotion?"

Holger said: "Devotion? Early on a Sunday morning the Druids take you to the top of a hill to honor the sun. You are given twelve little white rocks and a few words that only the priest knows. You lay the twelve stones in a circle with each one three steps away from the other. Every time a rock is placed you must speak the special words. The words must resound loudly and truly from the heart. You spread you arms wide, toward the sun, like a bowl. This is done with every stone. After you have completed the circle you lay down in the center for awhile. You press your hands and forehead into the ground as if you are a part of the earth itself. Then you feel the warmth penetrating your back. That is the love of the sun for the earth. The other exercises come after that but I don't know about them yet because they are only given to students who have completed the Sun Circle. If one completes all of these things satisfactorily, then one is accepted into the Druid School. If not, then one becomes a hunter, builder, or soldier. But, Gerwin, now I must ask something of you. You were very brave in bearing your pain so I told you these things. But, you understand, don't you, that it must remain just between us? This is not something that one normally speaks about with other people."

Gerwin took Holger's hand in his and replied: "I am glad we share this secret. May I be your friend, just like you are friends with Geron?"

Holger answered: "Maybe later I will make a blood pact with you, after I see that you show perseverance in the friendship. But right now, let's get some sleep! Soon the dewy, midnight spirits will be floating over the fields."

Not long after that Gerwin heard Holger's even breathing. He had hardly any pain left from the ant bites. He thought back on his experiences of this evening: first, burning pain and then Holger's new, wonderful friendship. From the distance he could hear a rooster's crow, two, three times, and then he fell asleep.

Wugo's Axes

The next morning, men and boys ate the rest of the warmed-up wolf soup with pieces of flat bread. German said: "We are five workers but we have only three axes. Geron, take your horse and ride to the old hunter, Wugo. He has four axes. They're hanging inside his hut on either side of the door. I saw them there not long ago. The last time we were together on a bear hunt I left the whole pelt for Wugo. So he owes me something. Give him my greetings and ask him to lend me one or two axes. He also has two older servants, Bor and Bur, and a Roman slave. Maybe he would also lend me one or the other to work with the ax."

Geron put a piece of bread and some sheep cheese into his leather pouch and said: "Will do, Father. I will come right back to the forest after I've been there."

As Geron was riding from the valley over the hill, he could see Wugo's hut and fields on the other side. Geron knew that Wugo and his wife, Runege, were rich with cattle but had no children of their own. They were not friendly with their own families because Runege had a sharp, evil tongue. Many thought of her as a witch. Geron rode down the other side of the hill. He could see a servant working alone in the field. He would ask him if Wugo was at home. He greeted the servant with a loud "Hali."

The servant was startled, but he did not return the greeting. Was this the Roman? Geron rode over to him. Yes, he could see that it was indeed the Roman slave of whom Holger had spoken. The chains were spanned between his feet. He had bound a dirty piece of cloth around his hips. He was hoeing the ground to prepare it for seeding. He looked mistrustfully at the approaching rider and put down the hoe.

Geron was amazed at his curly black hair and equally dark eyes. "Is Wugo at home?" Geron asked, without further greeting since a German does not greet a Roman slave.

The slave answered: "Wugo in house . . . foot sick." It was obvious he had trouble speaking the German language. He came two or three steps closer to Geron. The chains rattled.

Geron looked him in the eyes once again and suddenly, he was sorry for the boy. He was hardly older than Geron: "What is your name?"

The slave answered: "Wugo say Roman. My name is Virtus." Geron was probably the first person in Germany to ask him his name. Geron was silent and he again looked into the slave's eyes. The slave looked down, picked up his hoe, and said softly: "Work, or Wugo hit me." Geron reached into his pouch and took out a piece of bread and some of the cheese: "Here, Virtus, for you." The hoe dropped from the slave's hands. He slowly held up both of his dirt-stained hands to Geron, cupped them, and accepted the food in an almost ceremonial fashion. Geron noticed how his dark eyes lit up and heard how the slave uttered strange sounding words that he did not understand. Then Geron gave his horse a signal. It turned and started toward Wugo's farm.

Loud barking was Geron's welcome. Wugo had two dangerous dogs. One could not walk into their fenced area in front of the house unless the dogs were tied up. Runege came out of the hut and screamed at the dogs. They slunk into a corner, growling all the way. Bur and Bor, the two farmhands, hurried out of the stable to see what was going on.

Geron jumped off his horse, letting the animal graze where it was while he went through the gate. Runege walked up to him and croaked: "Well, look here, if it isn't German's son! What brings you here? Is someone sick at home? Should I help? Should I prepare a magic spell?"

Geron knew the old crone well and he gave her a short answer: "I'm here to see Wugo, with a message from Father."

"So come on then, come on, to poor Wugo. A tree trunk fell on his foot. Poor Wugo! But it serves him right, he didn't listen to me!" She grabbed Geron's arm with her spindly fingers and pulled him into the hut.

Wugo lay on a bearskin rug and one foot was wrapped in rags. He was happy to have the distraction of a visitor. Geron gave him a handshake as a greeting. Right away Wugo asked him: "How far along are you with the new house? Is the roof almost up?"

Geron explained that it was going more slowly than they had hoped: "Holding and his son Holger have come to help us. But we don't have enough good axes. My father wanted me to ask you if you could lend us two axes for a few days. It would make him very happy. He also remembered the bearskin and wondered if you could see fit to lend us one of your farmhands with an ax as well. I could take him back with me on the horse."

Wugo made a sour face. Geron asked quickly: "How is your foot? Is it very painful? Shall I ask Uralda for some herbs?"

Runege immediately interrupted: "We don't need any of Uralda's herbs! I wrapped his foot in fresh cow manure. That will do him good!" Runege said with a satisfied grin: "Yes, my cow manure is better than all of Uralda's herbs. The cows eat all of the herbs and they're all right there in the manure anyway!"

Geron brought the subject back around to the axes: "Now, Wugo, as I see by the door, you already have beautiful axes! May I have a closer look at them?"

Wugo said: "Yes, bring them here! I will tell you where I got them." Wugo gave a full report of which blacksmith had made which ax. One of them was Roman.

Finally Geron got up his courage and said: "Wugo, which two will you lend to us? They're getting rusty from disuse up there on the wall. We will sharpen them for you and polish them with river bottom sand and rub them with wolf fat."

Wugo asked in amazement: "With wolf fat? Are you kidding?" Now Geron had to tell him the whole wolf story. Wugo was an old hunter. When Geron told him how he had clubbed the wolf while riding his horse, Wugo sat upright and said: "Good, since you are a wolf hunter and you will bring the axes back sharpened, polished, and oiled, then you may borrow two for seven days. But Bur and Bor I cannot spare right now since I cannot work myself."

Geron suddenly had an idea. He very casually inquired: "And the Roman slave?"

Wugo said angrily: "That lazy animal! He won't help you. He's barely able to hoe and drive cattle. But Holding is strong. Maybe he can whip him enough that he'll work."

Geron said: "We'll get him to work. I can take him with me on my horse. He can chop branches even with the chains on his feet."

Wugo decided: "It's fine with me. You can borrow him for seven days. But see that he doesn't get away from you. He's worth three cows, and the chains are worth a steer."

Before Geron could ride away, Runege had to tie up the dogs. He stuck both axes in his belt, said his farewells, and rode back to the field where the Roman slave was working. When Geron got nearer, Virtus held up one hand and waved. The bread and cheese were much appreciated. Geron jumped off his horse and spoke to Virtus: "Leave the hoe. Bur and Bor will continue. Sit on my horse. I have borrowed you for seven days." He held up seven fingers.

The slave did not understand and shook his head: "Virtus not may go! Wugo hit!"

Geron tried again to explain: "Wugo says yes! I am your master for seven days. You are to work for me." Geron grabbed the leg chains and pointed to the horse: "Sit!"

Finally the Roman understood that the young rider was not just having fun, and he allowed himself to be helped upon the horse. He had to hold up his legs because the leg chains were a little too short. Virtus looked worriedly back at the hut to see if the dogs were coming, but nothing happened.

Geron wanted to bring the horse to a gallop so he ordered Virtus: "Hold on tightly to me!" The slave put his strong arms around Geron's middle at the same time holding the axes inside his belt to keep them from falling out. The horse began to gallop. Virtus still had no idea what was going to happen to him, but the further he got from Wugo's hut the happier he was because he trusted Geron. He had given him bread and cheese and told him his name.

Back at the forest the tree chopping was going full force. Just as the two boys rode up, a high pine tree crashed to the ground. Everyone ran up to see Wugo's axes as well as the slave. German asked: "Wouldn't Wugo give you a servant who isn't in chains? That won't work very well for chopping down trees."

Geron answered: "No, Wugo is sick. He wanted to keep Bur and Bor with him. But look at the Roman's muscles! They will surely make the ax sing."

German said: "We'll find out right now. He can start by chopping the branches off this fallen pine. Give him Wugo's Roman ax!" Virtus soon understood what he had to do here. Geron gave him encouragement, and Virtus went to it with such a passion that the wood chips were flying.

Gerwin and Holger, who were working on another tree, saw that the Roman was faster than both of them combined. Geron walked up to him and said: "Virtus, well done! You are strong!" His dark Roman eyes were sparkling with joy. It was the first praise he had heard in one year of enslavement.

Only Holding behaved badly as far as the Roman slave was concerned. He said: "I hate all Romans! They killed my father. The slave shall not eat out of the same bowl as we do."

Gerda and Ina brought the midday meal which consisted of porridge with pieces of wolf meat in it. There was no spoon for Virtus. Geron got a large piece of tree bark, put some of the food on it, and brought it to Virtus. He had to sit alone on a pile of branches and eat with his fingers. German said the blessing and the meal began. Once in a while Geron would look over at Virtus, but he seemed content to eat by himself.

They had never before gotten so much wood over to the building site in one day. When it was evening and quitting time, Holding said: "Starting tomorrow German and I will be working only on the construction. The boys can work alone now at felling the trees and bringing the wood to the building site. Geron knows what he is doing and the Roman is useful."

That evening on the way home German said to his son, Geron: "The Roman can eat and sleep in the sheep stable. Holding will not sleep under the same roof as a Roman."

So Geron brought Virtus to the stable. He spread out some straw in a corner and warned him: "Virtus, do not go outside at night. Waldo, the dog, would bark and bite. He is very watchful at night."

Holger's Second Bedtime Story

In the winter the cows were brought inside German's house and so there was not a lot of sleeping space. But in the summer and late into autumn the animals stayed outside until the first frost. So right now there was room and fresh straw aplenty. Gerda heard from Gerwin that Holger had told him an interesting bedtime story the night before. She said: "Tonight Geron and I want to hear Holger's story too. I put some hay and straw into the farthest corner for us tonight. We won't disturb anyone there."

When it was time for bed that night suddenly there was thunder in the distance. Uralda limped to the doorway, lay her hands on the door posts and murmured these words:

> Thor – Tyr, flash in lightning,
> Flash a zig zag to Jotunheim.
> Flash your fire down to the earth!
> Protect this house, protect the coals!
> Lend your protection to us and the animals!

She repeated these words over and over again, sometimes loud and sometimes soft. She waved at Gerda to come over to her so she could also speak the protective, magic lightning words.

Outside the storm was approaching with loud thunder. Suddenly Geron ran out the door. He was holding something under his arm. He hurried to the sheep stable. Just then a streak of lightning lit up the sky.

Then he saw the Roman slave crouching in a corner. "Virtus, here is a goat skin for you." He threw it in the corner. The chains rattled. When lightning once again lit up the sky Geron saw how Virtus pushed the straw that was still dry under him, rolled up into a ball and covered up with the goat skin. The first rain drops were already falling. Geron hurried back to the house. Gerda and Uralda were still quietly murmuring their magic words.

It was raining very hard now and the thunder was deafening. Holger whispered to Gerwin: "Do you hear how the gods are fighting the giants?" Everyone listened to the overpowering event in silent awe.

Finally the thunder rolled past them and the rain began to let up. Uralda went to her sleeping place. Gerda went back to her brothers. Everyone went to sleep. Gerwin asked: "Holger, do you know a story about the god of lightning?"

Holger replied: "Yes, it is about Thor and his lightning hammer, Mjolnir. I will tell it to you just the way I heard it from Evart the Druid.

Thor is able to fight the storm giants with his hammer. Every time he smashes his hammer onto a giant's skull during a storm fight, Mjolnir always returns to his hands. One morning as Thor awakened he felt for his hammer in the place he had left it before he went to sleep. His hand felt only empty space. Mjolnir was gone—stolen. Thor became very angry and thought: 'One of the storm giants must have taken it while I was sleeping. This is terrible. If I don't have my hammer in my hand anymore against the giants, I cannot protect the gods' castle, Valhalla.' He went to the cunning and crafty god, Loki, and said: 'My hammer was stolen this night. Help me search for it!'

Loki promised to help. He flew down into the kingdom of the giants, to Jotunheim. He found the king of the giants, Thrym, sitting on top of a hill and grinning. Loki thought at once: 'That is the thief!' He asked Thrym: 'Did you happen to find Thor's hammer?' The giant answered: 'Yes, I have it! It is sunk so deep in the earth that no god's eye can find it. If Thor wants it back, then you gods will have to give me Freya, goddess of beauty, as a bride.'

Loki returned to Valhalla with this message and there was much anger among the gods. The wise Heimdall took the initiative and said: 'We must find a way to trick Thrym. Thor, put on clothes like Freya and make yourself up to look like her. Put a concealing veil over your face. Loki, take on the form of a servant. When Thrym brings the hammer to exchange for his bride, you know what to do.'

At first Thor was not willing to go along with this plan. He grumbled: 'What, I should dress up as a woman?' But he allowed himself to be persuaded. After all, this was about his hammer!

At about this time Thrym was overseeing the preparations at his castle to receive his goddess bride. A huge wedding feast was prepared. There were fish and roasted ox and brewed drinks in enormous pots.

When the beautifully dressed, though rather large, bride appeared with her servant, Thrym immediately invited them to the banquet table. He wanted to wait until after the feast to get the hammer. He was amazed at the enormous pieces of meat that his bride was able to put down her throat and the way she downed large mugs of brew underneath her veil. Thrym grinned: 'I'm getting a wife who can eat and drink with the best of the giants. This is going to be a great wedding!' All the other giants and their wives who were taking part in the wedding feast were astounded over the appetite and thirst of the bride. Thrym was so excited that he lifted Freya's veil just a little in order to give her a kiss. Two angry, fire-blazing eyes stared back at him. He was so shocked that he quickly let the veil fall back into place. He asked: 'How can a woman's gaze be so fiery hot?'

But before his distrust could take hold, Loki quickly interjected: 'Freya was so longing to be in the giants' kingdom that she did not sleep for many nights. That is why her eyes are burning so.'

The giant was happy with that explanation and he grumbled: 'It's a good wife who can eat and drink as much as she.' He ordered a servant to fetch the hammer from its hiding place deep in a crevice of the earth. Mountain trolls were sent out to carry it up from the depths. Thrym lay the hammer in his bride's lap.

Immediately, the hammer Mjolnir clung fast to Thor's hand. He tore off the veil. Fiery darts of lightning shot out of his eyes. He held the hammer high and thrust it down hard onto Thrym's skull. There was a cracking noise that sounded like a boulder had been split asunder. The hammer robber fell down dead. Those of the guests who were unable to flee also had their skulls cracked by Mjolnir. That is how Thor got revenge for the giant's evil act and, from that day forward, the giants were very shy about going after the gods.'

Holger had finished his story. Geron said: "One time I saw a huge, old oak tree. It had been hit by Thor's lightening hammer. There were split branches lying all around and the trunk was split right down the middle. Thor must be the most powerful of all the gods!"

Gerda, who was half asleep, asked: "Is Freya really the most beautiful of all the goddesses?"

And Holger answered: "It must be so since she is called the goddess of beauty. Maybe you will see her sometime in your dreams and she will give you some of her beauty as a gift."

It had finally stopped raining and even Virtus had fallen asleep under his goat skin.

The Ride to Evart the Druid

The leaves on the trees had begun to turn their autumn colors. The Roman slave, Virtus, was long ago sent back to Wugo. German and his sons were allowed to use the two axes a while longer. Holding and Holger had returned to their farm. The frame of the new log house was up. Soon the finishing work could begin. German went to the marsh pond to cut rushes. The boys tied them into tight bundles and carried them on their backs to the log house. One day German said to Geron: "Soon it will be full moon. Take your horse and ride to Holding's farm. Holger can show you the way to the Druids. Go to the Druid Evart and ask if he will come to bless the new house at the full moon."

Geron started off early the next morning. It was a long ride through the forest to Holger's house. It would have taken half a day on foot. In the distance Geron could see Holding's large house, and he noticed the sheep and cows were grazing in the pasture. He thought: "Maybe Holger is watching them." He wanted to surprise him so he rode around the hill in order to come closer to the herd unnoticed.

Suddenly he heard someone singing. He dismounted and tied the horse to a tree. Geron listened. It was not Holger's voice. Could it be his sister, Helga? Holger had told him that his sister knew many songs and even composed some of her own. Geron walked slowly toward the sound. He hid behind a bush and saw Helga as he peeked through the branches. She was sitting on a big rock. She was holding a lamb in her lap and singing. She had made a crown of colorful autumn leaves and put it in her hair. Geron did not wish to startle her. He lay down on the ground and listened. He understood some of the words.

She was singing about a water fairy who was longing to be with people. The fairy was in love with a shepherd and wanted to bring him down into her water world. Helga had a high, bright voice and it seemed as if she was singing to the little lamb she held in her lap. The song ended. Geron whistled the melody of a blackbird.

Helga stopped, got up, and slowly walked toward the bush to get a better look at the hidden bird. Geron did not move. Suddenly Helga gave a hearty laugh: "Geron, is that you? I thought it was strange that a blackbird would be singing on an autumn afternoon. Have you come for a visit? Does your father need more help for the house?"

Geron answered: "No, I came to see Holger. He is supposed to show me the way to Evart the Druid. We are going to have the house-warming at the full moon. You are all invited. We are going to slaughter an ox, offer a sacrifice, and play games. Then you can sing that song that I just heard for everyone."

Helga shook her head: "I don't like to sing in front of other people. I sing for the sheep, the flowers, and the invisible ones."

Geron nodded: "Do you mean me? I was also invisible just now."

Helga agreed: "Yes, for you and Holger I can sing because you can both listen in silence. Holger came to pick me up yesterday evening. It was getting dark when I sang the evening song. Suddenly he saw a whole group of gnomes here on the hill. Elves were doing a dance in the air. I couldn't see them myself, but Holger can see such things. He has a light soul. I don't see the invisible ones but I can feel their presence. Can you see them, Geron?"

"No, I have an earthy soul. I am a hunter and a destroyer of wolves. I don't see them, but I know that they are there. Holger has told me quite a lot about them, and I know he tells the truth. Well, I must ride on. The sun is going towards midday. Holger is at home, isn't he?"

"Yes, he is helping Father repair the stable. It was nice that you were here, Geron." Once again on his horse, Geron looked back and saw Helga waving goodbye. He urged his horse to go faster and leaned deep into the horse's mane until his blond, wavy hair seemed to become a part of the mane blowing in the wind.

Holding greeted Geron jovially: "Here comes my wolf killer! What brings you here?"

Geron replied: "My father invites the entire Holding family to our housewarming at the next full moon! Can you spare Holger to show me the way to Evart the Druid? I must take him the message from Father asking him to prepare the sacrifice."

Holding responded gladly: "Our repair work is soon finished. The rest I can do by myself. Holger, get your horse!"

Just at that moment Holger's younger brother, Hoegge, shot out of the house. He called out: "Wait, wait! I want to go with you! I haven't ridden on Geron's horse in the longest time."

Geron looked at Holding, who laughed, shrugged his shoulders, and remarked: "Whatever you decide, Geron." Hoegge was already hanging on one of Geron's legs.

Geron said: "If you can sit astride the horse by yourself, then you can come with me." At these words, Hoegge pulled so hard on Geron's leg that Geron lost his balance and slid off the horse. Geron only laughed and lifted Hoegge up on the horse's back. Hoegge triumphantly waved his arms in the air. Holding was laughing so hard that he dropped his ax. Mother Hulda and Grandfather Helge came outside to see what all the commotion was about. Geron jumped up on his horse again, behind Hoegge, and rode off. Holger followed on his own horse.

Holding mirthfully remarked to his wife, Hulda: "I wonder what kind of mischief Hoegge will get into today?"

The way to Evart the Druid led through forests and clearings until they came to a ridge. High cliffs broke through the forest. A small lake was tucked into the landscape like a blue-green eye. Holger pointed to the other side of the lake: "Look, over there is the Druid's farm! Many Druids live there together with their students. They plant crops and raise cattle. They raise fish in the lake and they also keep bees for the honey and wax for candles. You can see their white horses on the pasture over there between the trees.

"But Evart is a hermit. He makes his home in a little cave up there in the cliff face. Sometimes, if it is very cold in the winter, he will live down here on the farm for a little while. Geron, you can tie your horse to this tree. We'll walk up to Evart's cave."

Hoegge, who was rather short and slightly chubby, protested: "I want to stay down here by the water so I can throw rocks and look at the fish."

Holger agreed he could stay: "All right, stay here, but don't wander off and don't bother the horse!"

A little way up the path they came to two large oak trees and could clearly see the path to the cliffs winding upward between the trees. They had just started up some stone steps when a raven flew down and, to Geron's astonishment, landed on Holger's shoulder. It was the Druid's tame raven. It knew Holger and Holger called it by its name, Hugi. Hugi cawed, grabbed a hunk of Holger's hair with its beak, and shook his head back and forth. Holger called up to the cave: "Is Father Evart here?"

From above the answer came: "Holger, come on up!" Evart had recognized his voice. Holger walked up with the raven still perched on his shoulder. Geron saw Evart for the first time standing at the top of the stone steps. He was middle-aged and wore his hair hanging loose over his shoulders. But his hair was cut away in a circle at the top of his head so that his forehead seemed to protrude. He wore a long, white robe. The raven flew to Evart's outstretched arm and cawed again as if to say: "Visitors, visitors!" The Druid greeted Holger by laying his hands on both of Holger's shoulders.

Holger said: "This is my friend, Geron, of whom I have told you much." Evart also put his hands on Geron's shoulders and looked long into his eyes. Geron could not look away. It seemed as if the Druid was looking deep into his soul. It suddenly occurred to Geron why Holger's gaze was so earnest. There was something of Evart's light in Holger's eyes. With a loud caw, the raven suddenly flew up and away.

Evart invited both of his visitors to come inside the cave where he lived. It was high and partly built up with stones at the entrance. The only light came from the door opening. There was a small fire flickering inside and the smoke rose up and out a small niche above. A three-legged pot was standing over the coals. A smell of herbs was coming from the pot. There were strange symbols hanging on the walls, and a skull could be dimly seen on a niche on the wall. Geron shivered a bit as he looked around. At the back of the cave there was a massive bearskin rug spread on the floor. That must be where Evart sleeps, thought Geron.

Evart took a seat upon the bearskin rug and indicated to his guests to take a seat upon wooden stools nearby. Evart asked: "What brings you here, my sons?"

Holger signaled Geron that he should speak, which he did: "Greetings and honor from my father, German! He wishes to ask if you would come and bless our new house on the next full moon. And, if so, would you please tell us what preparations must be made."

Evart answered: "How wonderful, you've built a new house! What a lot of work! We will certainly ask for the gods' protection. Yes, we must! Full moon is in seven days. Yes, I can come. You must fasten a small pine branch over the house entrance and in the middle of the house a small, young ash tree. A fire site surrounded by stones should be made twelve large paces away from the door. Wood for the fire should be prepared from pine, ash, and oak. I will bring herbs and pine resin with me. Jugs of water should be at hand. Have a ram ready for sacrifice. The blessing ceremony will begin with sunrise and last until the sun's highest point at midday. The thatch for the roof should be ready, and with everyone's help the roof should be finished by evening. I will stay with you the first night. The first hearth fire in the house will be lit from the sacrificial fire. Make sure that early in the morning of the blessing ceremony your whole family washes themselves in the river close to the house." The Druid thought for a moment and then went on: "And now, my son Geron, repeat everything I have told you."

Geron had listened very carefully. He repeated everything from the beginning exactly as Evart had told him. Evart stood up and served both boys cups of herb tea. The smell of thyme rose into Geron's nose. Evart said with a laugh: "The flowers in the tea give one good thoughts."

Geron's gaze went once again to the skull on the wall. The Druid saw it and spoke: "Every person carries life and death inside of him. The skull should remind us to make something good out of our lives." Evart was silent. They all three drank the rest of their tea in silence.

Geron looked around again, his eyes finally coming to rest on the high forehead of the Druid. He thought: "When I am older I would like to ask Evart about many things in this world that puzzle me."

Holger interrupted the silence: "Geron, we should go now so that you can find your way back home before nightfall. Where did Hugi go? I wanted to say goodbye to him."

Evart said: "Oh, he often flies down to the lake. When one of the brothers is fishing they give Hugi a little fish to eat."

Evart said farewell to the boys as ceremoniously as he had greeted them. Then they began their walk back down to the lake. The horse was there but Hoegge was nowhere in sight. Holger called him. There was no answer. Geron said: "He couldn't have fallen in the water. He would have jumped out faster than he fell in!"

Holger surmised: "Hoegge loves horses. Perhaps he went to look at the white horses. We'll ride over there." They mounted and rode toward the Druid farm. The horse pasture was overgrown with many bushes and small trees. The horses could roam free there. Sheep were also grazing.

Suddenly Holger cried: "Look there! It's Hoegge." Hoegge was trying to ride a sheep. He had a hunk of wool in one hand and in the other hand he was holding a raven that was cawing hysterically and fluttering its wings.

Geron let out a loud whistle. The sheep tore off running and Hoegge fell on his bottom, but he managed to keep the raven held fast in his fist. Holger jumped off the horse and over the fence, rushing toward Hoegge. The raven began furiously pecking Hoegge. "Let go of the raven!"

Hoegge stubbornly refused: "No, I caught him and I'm going to take him home with me."

Holger grabbed his hand and ordered him to let go: "His name is Hugi and he belongs to Evart the Druid." Hoegge opened his mouth in surprise and let Holger take the frightened bird. He smoothed its feathers, talked to it in a soft, friendly voice, and then let it fly away.

Hoegge lamented: "It's really too bad. I had just made such good friends with it. The horses wouldn't let me sit on them. But I was almost able to ride the ram, if the stupid whistle hadn't sounded."

After a little while the three started the ride home. In the evening Geron could report to his father everything that would be required for the house blessing ceremony. Gerwin and Gerda were impressed by Hoegge's shenanigans. They asked: "Is Hoegge also coming to the housewarming? That would be great!" German said: "Why should he not come? A little fun wouldn't hurt!"

The Housewarming

In the evening two days before full moon, German's family sat around the fire in the old house. Geron and his father were sharpening Wugo's two axes with flat stones. They had promised to return them sharp and polished. Ina was spinning wool. Suddenly she said: "Should we not also invite Wugo and his wife Runege to the housewarming? His axes have been of good service to us. Without them we would not be having the ceremony the day after tomorrow."

Uralda replied: "I don't trust Runege. She might bring some black magic into our new house. She ate wolf's tongue! I believe she is in touch with evil spirits. She might ruin our sacrifice."

German spoke: "We cannot ignore Wugo. It is better to be on good terms with him. His axes really were a tremendous help to us. Maybe he will not even bring Runege with him. She's always on him about something the whole day long. Geron, ride over to Wugo's place early in the morning. Return the axes. Tell him thanks and invite him, in my name, to our housewarming."

Geron said: "What should I say if Runege wants to come as well?"

German said: "I do not think she will invite herself. That goes against all good manners."

Ina added: "Tell her that when the house has a roof and is completely finished inside I would be happy to have a visit from her. That way she can satisfy her curiosity."

The next morning as Geron was nearing Wugo's house, he spotted Virtus. He was working on fixing the fence around the house. Joy was in the slave's eyes when he saw Geron and heard Geron call out his name. Virtus asked: "You bring axes. House finished?"

Geron understood and said: "The day after tomorrow the roof goes up, Virtus. Maybe I can take you to it sometime so you can see it for yourself."

Virtus also understood what Geron had said and replied: "Geron, you only person good to me. I sometime tell you much about Roman people."

Geron asked: "Where is Wugo?"

Virtus replied: "Wugo in house. I come with, then dogs good." So Geron tied his horse to a fence post and went with Virtus through the gate. The dogs perked up their ears and barked, but when Virtus commanded them to stop, they lay back down and were silent.

The short barking was enough, however, to draw the curious Runege to the doorway. When she saw Geron she waddled up to him: "My strong, my handsome Geron, do you bring clean axes back?" She lay her hand on his shoulder in a familiar manner and tried to usher him through the door.

But Geron resisted: "I don't have time to be your guest today." At that moment Wugo appeared. He took the axes and carefully examined them, testing their sharpness with his thumb.

Geron said: "My father sends his heartfelt thanks for the axes. They were of good service to us. Because of them the house is ready for the roof thatching and blessing ceremony tomorrow. As Father's hunting companion, Wugo, you are invited to the festivities tomorrow."

Runege made a long face and pursed her lips as if she wanted to say something. But she did not. Geron then turned to the old woman and said: "My mother, Ina, sends greetings to you, Runege. You are invited to visit her at the new house in one week when everything is finished and ready for visitors."

Runege smiled her sweet-sour smile and answered: "I'll come. I'll bring herbs."

Wugo said: "I'll go hunting today. Hopefully I will bring some fresh meat as a gift. Geron, would you like to come along on the hunt?"

Geron answered: "I can't right now. You know how much preparation is yet to be done before tomorrow." Wugo understood. Geron said his farewells.

When Geron returned to his horse, Virtus had already untied it for him. He spoke softly: "Geron, I not forget. Wugo ordered Bur and Bor whip me. Two days can't walk." Tears were in his eyes as he spoke. When Geron was once again on his horse, Virtus grabbed his leg and kissed his foot.

Geron thought: "That must be some kind of Roman custom." For the first time Geron offered his handshake to Virtus and said: "Virtus, I will not forget you and I will show you the house sometime." He signaled his horse and galloped away toward home.

At home everyone was hard at work. Father called to Geron: "Come, help me build the stone altar for the sacrificial fire. It goes faster with two! I have already measured the twelve paces."

Geron and German had finished the hearth in the house the day before. They had used some stones from the old hearth to mix in with the new because the old one had been blessed for such a long time. Gerwin was given the task of getting the pine branch for the door, and Gerda was to cut down a small ash tree. Geron climbed up and fastened both into place.

Now it was time to slaughter the ox for the feast. The women and Gerda cooked ox-blood soup and put the meat onto three different spits. It was now all ready to roast on the following day. Gerwin carried in wood for the fire. Afterward, he hung up pieces of meat on the rafters in the old house above the hearth so the meat would be preserved by the smoke. He used lengths of washed intestines from the ox to tie up the meat. The skin of the animal would be rubbed with oak ashes and stretched over a tree trunk. It would be a gift for Evart the Druid.

Days ago Uralda had put barley kernels, herbs, roots, and berries into a pail of water to brew a festive drink. The whole family was busy until late into the night. Finally, everyone was sitting around the fire in the old house sipping ox-blood soup. Gerda asked sadly: "And what will happen to our good old house? I can't even feel happy about the new house for thinking about the old one."

Uralda answered her: "It will take some time until all the good spirits in the old house move over to the new house. But when that happens the new house will also have a soul. Our animals will be able to stay in the old house in the winter. That will protect them from the cold. Then we will have much more room in the new house and will be able to keep it very clean without the animals inside. The old house was built by my grandfather. The winter snow fell on the roof about one hundred times. But the god's lightning hammer always protected it. We want to bring this blessing to the new house as well. For today, let us rest peacefully under the gods' protection!" Uralda tossed a spoonful of the blood soup into the coals and murmured her words of blessing.

After such a hard day's work, one after the other began to drop off to sleep. Geron thought back on how Virtus had said farewell to him that day. What all could he tell him about the Romans? He had heard they built their houses out of stone, even the ones for their gods.

Uralda awakened everyone before sunrise. It had been their last night's sleep in the old house. She took some water from a bowl that had been placed next to the fire all night and sprinkled some on everyone's face.

When he got up, Geron remembered that the wolf's skull that he had long ago taken from the anthill was not yet fastened above the door of the new house. He had carefully wrapped it inside a rabbit pelt and stored it in a trunk. He fetched it and made his way to the new house. It was just the beginning of dawn. After he had hung the skull in its proper place over the door he went to the sheep stable and fetched the ram which German had designated for the sacrifice and tied him to a post next to the altar. German and Geron stacked wood for the sacrificial fire.

When the women returned from their wash in the river, German and his sons went for theirs. The morning light in the east was strengthening. The bathing was barely finished when they heard a multi-voiced "Haliii!"

Geron and Gerwin yelled back: "Hallooo!" So it went back and forth for a while. In the bright dawn Geron suddenly saw the white horse of the Druid. Holding was riding next to him. The others were following on foot.

Geron thought: "They must have started out shortly after midnight." The Druid was sitting very straight on his horse and once again wearing a white robe. When Evart dismounted Geron noticed that he wore a symbol on his chest that was made of some kind of shiny metal. It looked like a wheel. It must be his symbol of the priesthood.

German was the first to greet Evart. They laid their hands on each other's shoulders and exchanged words of friendship. Then Geron greeted Evart. Evart said to him: "The strength of Thor be with you!"

To Gerwin he said: "May Odin give you wisdom!" To Gerda he said: "May Freya give you grace and peace!" He greeted Uralda and Ina with the words: "My dear sisters of domesticity."

German and his family formed a half-circle around the fire with their eyes toward the house. The Holdings completed the circle. Grandfather Helge had stayed at home to care for the animals. Holding had told little Hoegge that he must behave today. That is why Hoegge was trying very hard to remain quiet. He pressed his lips together in concentration.

Geron looked out toward the field to see if Wugo was coming. He was not in sight. Perhaps he was just late.

Evart the Druid began to speak: "Since we have gathered here today to bless this house let us now return to the old house to bring some of its fire to this sacrificial altar. Everyone follow me!" He took his long, carved staff. First came German and his family followed by the Holdings. When they reached the old house Evart knocked three times on the threshold with his staff before he entered the house and walked to the dimly flickering hearth fire. Everyone formed a circle around the fire.

The Druid spoke: "Uralda, Ina! Keepers of the hearth, take the burning coals!" The women used two pieces of wood to shove some of the coals into a bowl. Evart handed Holger his staff, took the bowl in both hands and said: "We ask that the good spirits of this hearth move with us into the new house!" He walked toward the door with the bowl. He put the bowl down on the threshold for a moment and repeated: "We ask that the good spirits of this hearth move with us into the new house!"

Now Evart carried the bowl toward the new house. Holger was at his side carrying the staff. Everyone else followed behind. At that moment the first rays of sunrise came fully into view. The Druid began to sing a strange song that repeated these words over and over: "Light of fire – Brilliance of the gods!"

When they reached the place of sacrifice, Evart shook the coals into the kindling wood that was already prepared. He smiled and winked at little Hoegge and signaled that he should approach the Druid. He told Hoegge: "Blow the breath of man into the coals!" Hoegge did not need to be told twice. The ashes flew in his eyes. He paid no attention but kept on blowing and blowing. Soon the fire began to flicker and blaze. The Druid gave a sign. Hoegge stopped blowing. Everyone got on their knees and, facing the fire, opened their arms in prayer. The smoke rose to the heavens.

The Druid stood still. He raised one hand, pointing toward the sun, and with the other hand he pointed toward the fire and began to speak:

> Sun of the gods, eternal brilliance!
> Light of the heavenly Baldur!
> We give you thanks!
> You chase away the nightly darkness.
> We give you thanks for the life
> that allows everything to become and grow!
> We give you thanks for the love
> that warms all beings!
> Sun of the gods, eternal brilliance!
> Give of your strength for this fire,
> Radiate your power into this new house!

Evart took the staff and made a sign in the air and one in the smoke of the fire. Then he tossed pine resin and herbs into the flames. Everyone remained in silent meditation. Evart asked them all to repeat each line of the Sun Verse after him. And they did.

When the last line had been spoken: "Radiate your power into this new house!" Hoegge whispered: "The mouse, too!"

The Druid added: "So be it!" Everyone stood up.

Evart pointed to the sacrificial ram who was chewing his last bit of grass. German brought him around. The Druid spoke soft, friendly words to the young ram. A quick, painless cut of the knife and the animal sacrificed his blood into the fire bowl.

Afterward the Druid washed his hands in a bowl of water prepared for that purpose. More wood was added to the fire and the ram was laid over the flames as a sacrifice to the gods. Evart sprinkled some of the ram's blood from the bowl into the fire with a pine branch. He passed the branch to each person so they could do the same starting with German's family and then the Holdings.

Last of all was little Hoegge's turn. He wanted to do an especially good job. He dipped the branch deep into the bowl and when he pulled it out he sprayed blood all over his hair before sprinkling the rest in the fire. No one laughed or made a sound. Mother Hulda discreetly pointed to the bowl of water. Hoegge kneeled down and stuck his whole head into the water and washed himself blond again.

As the fire was crackling, Evart spoke words of sacrifice into the smoke. He thanked the spirits of the earth, water, air, and fire. Once more three kinds of wood were laid on the fire; pine, ash, and oak. After a few moments Evart spoke again: "Now we will bring some of the sacrificial fire into the new hearth." He took a burning stick and carried it like a torch. The whole procession followed him. He took twelve measured steps to the house, knocked on the threshold three times with his staff and entered.

Everyone again formed a circle around the hearth. The Druid circled the hearth three times and put the burning stick into the new hearth. This time Gerda and Helga were allowed to blow on the fire until it burst into flames. The first fire in the new house was lit! The Druid spoke a house blessing.

Suddenly, from outside, one could hear the hoof beats of a horse. Hoegge ran outside. Wugo had come late, just as the ceremonial part of the festivities had ended. There was a rabbit tied to his saddle whose pelt had already been removed. It had hopped in front of Wugo's arrow just this morning. Wugo was brimming over with excitement: "I'm late. I wanted to make the rabbit ready for roasting." It was assumed by everyone that he had skinned the rabbit at home so he could keep the pelt.

German thanked him: "A fresh rabbit brings luck. Thank you, Wugo!"

Hoegge offered his services: "I know how to roast a rabbit on a spit. Father taught me."

They all looked at Holding who nodded: "Yes, he really does know how." So Hoegge was given the rabbit to roast next to the ox meat on the sacrificial fire.

Geron was looking after the ox meat. They were not allowed to eat the meat of the sacrifice. It slowly burned until it was black and coal-like. The girls would soon relieve Geron from roasting duty so that he could help the others thatch the roof. The hearth fire inside the house was covered completely with ashes so that the smoke would not disturb those working on the roof.

Holding and German got onto the roof. The women bound the rushes into small bundles. Gerwin, Holger, and Geron climbed up and down the rafters to bring up the bundles of thatch. The two fathers fastened the bundles so that soon the roof had a thick coat of thatch from the bottom to the top. Even Wugo climbed up onto the roof although his leg was not yet completely healed. His task was to carefully form the smoke hole and make sure it was well padded.

While the roasting meat was only sitting on the coals, Uralda sent the girls to help with the thatching. But she did not allow Hoegge to be disturbed while he roasted the rabbit. Sometimes he would give a yank on a back leg of the rabbit that was already roasted brown. He thought that was fun. Whenever Uralda was not looking, he tugged and pulled on the leg until it came off. He situated the spit a little higher away from the coals and disappeared behind a bush. Then he smacked and chewed away at the meat until it was all in his round little tummy. Oh, was it good! He stuck the bones into his little leather pouch. Nobody had noticed. Evart had gone into the forest looking for herbs.

The sun had already climbed to its midday height. Everyone gathered around for the feast. Evart had returned from the forest. Mother Ina was cutting the meat into pieces with a large knife and putting it into a large, clay bowl. She wanted to do the same with the rabbit meat but Hoegge vehemently protested: "I will do that myself; Father showed me how!" Ina gave him the knife and Hoegge cut up the meat. He swiped a bit of the ox meat out the bowl every so often when no one was looking. Then he took the rabbit bones out of his pouch, pressed them into the rest of the ox-rabbit mixture and said to himself: "There, the rabbit is whole again!" Evart blessed the food.

Wugo said: "Let's have the rabbit as an appetizer! Allow me to divide the four legs. The front ones go to Ina and Uralda." He searched in the bowl and laid them into the women's hands. "Holding and German get the two hind legs." Hoegge's face got red. Wugo found one hind leg right away, but could not find the other. He said: "For heaven's sake, Hoegge, where is the fourth leg?"

Hoegge replied: "I'll find it. It kind of fell apart when I was cutting it up. Here it is!" He pulled out the rabbit bone with ox meat on it: "Uh, the meat fell off the bone."

Wugo looked at it: "Well, there's the rabbit leg all right. Give it to your father." Hoegge gave Holding the rabbit-ox meat. Fortunately, the ox meat stuck fast to the rabbit bone so that Holding thought nothing more of the strange taste than that the rabbit had been a little old.

The First Night in the New House

The roof thatchers worked hard the whole afternoon and by evening the new house had a warm roof. Since Evart was staying the night in the house, the Holdings also decided to stay overnight.

But Wugo declared: "I have to get home and look to my Roman slave. I believe he is having thoughts of escape. He already tried to break his chains with one of my axes. I had Bur and Bor whip him until his blood flowed. Now I have to lock him up with the swine every night. Someday I will sell him." But Wugo was just using the slave as an excuse to get home. He did not like Druids. Years ago a Druid judge had found him guilty of horse beating. They took away both of his horses for half a year.

German thanked Wugo for his help with the roof and for the rabbit. As soon as Wugo was gone Geron thought how everyone seemed much more at ease.

Before the evening meal, Evart once again tossed some pine resin and herbs into the hearth fire and blessed the meal. Everyone took their places around the fire and began to eat. Uralda's special drink was passed around in two jugs. Fresh hay and straw from the summer cutting had already been brought into the house, as well as the animal skin rugs from the old house.

It was dark outside after the meal. Evart invited them all to come outside. He wanted to show them star constellations. Hoegge complained: "If I want to look up I have to lay on my back; otherwise I'll crack my neck." He immediately lay down on the ground.

Evart began: "The light of the world of the gods radiates from the stars. They make their way around the sky on a silent course. One single star always stays in the same place. It is Heaven's nail, the Resting Star." He pointed up at the constellation known as the Big

Dipper which he also called Seven Stars. He showed them how one could locate two other stars from the Resting Star. Everyone gazed up at the sky.

Suddenly, Hoegge yelled: "From where I am all the stars are resting stars. None of them is moving!"

Holger answered him: "You must not think that the stars are as restless as you or that they fly around like birds! Just observe for a little while toward the east where the sun rises in the morning. New stars are always appearing." All eyes turned to the east.

Suddenly Hoegge yelled again: "One is coming! It's a red one!"

Evart said: "Look closely. His light does not twinkle and blink. It is the fire star of the god Tyr. He sends light to the earth that brings us some of his strength."

Holger whispered to Geron: "Let his light shine on your hands!" And Geron did as Holger said and for a moment he greeted Tyr's star with the palms of his hands.

Evart pointed to the constellations of the Dragon and the Dragon Slayer. He said: "The gods must always fight against the Dragon."

Suddenly a falling star appeared and Hoegge said: "Finally, one of those stars really moved!"

Evart replied: "Yes, the spark of a god's sword! Strong human souls travel to earth on such paths of light and grow into being under their mother's heart. Other souls travel over the rainbow bridge. But let us now return to the house. Tonight I will tell you a long story."

On the way back to the house, Hoegge took hold of Evart's hand. Quietly, so the others could not hear, he asked: "Is my soul from the stars? Grandfather told me once that I have the soul of a frog and that is why I must always jump into everything and hop around like a frog."

Evart replied: "Grandfather was only having some fun with you. Your soul has also come from the stars. That is why your eyes shine so bright and fresh into the world." Hoegge did not let go of Evart's hand. And he spoke hardly a word the rest of the evening. For the first time in his life he was thinking about himself and his soul.

Everyone sat down in a circle in order to hear Evart's story. Evart was the only one who took a wooden stool by the fire. In the dim light Hoegge crawled out of the straw toward Evart and lay his head on Evart's knee just as Evert began to tell the story.

The Story of Odhr

Since the beginning of time the gods have lived in the bright, heavenly world known as *Asgard*. Their castle, *Valhalla*, radiates golden light. *Odin*, the father of all, sits there on his throne. His two ravens Hugir and Munir fly onto his shoulders and tell him what is going on in the human world. Then they fly back to earth and return again with news. But Odin often goes himself to the earth and, invisible, wanders around amongst the people.

The gods named the human kingdom *Midgard*, the garden of the middle. Underneath it, in the depths, is found the kingdom of the dark spirits. It is called *Schwartzalfaheim* or *Hel*. Giants, monsters, and terrifying creatures live there. They wish to entice people over to the dark side and blacken their souls. But now I will tell you the story of the god *Odhr* who got to know all three worlds.

Odhr had a wonderful voice and was a heavenly singer. When he sang in Valhalla all the gods and goddesses listened in attentive silence because whatever he sang in sound and words became visible to the gods. If he sang about the sun, moon, and stars, then their light would shine in the gods' souls. If he sang about Valhalla, then the rooms and halls would resound. Odhr sang about the rainbow,

Bifrost, which floated between heaven and earth in seven colors. He sang about the trees of the earth, the strong oak, the linden, and the dark pine. He sang about the twittering birds in the air and the glittering fish in the water. There was no wonder in the world that was not included in one of Odhr's songs. When Odhr sang, the storms of the earth would quiet and crawl back into the mountains. The sea became calmer and the waves smoother.

One time Odin had just returned to Valhalla from Midgard. He went to the earth disguised as an unknown traveler, which he often did. When he entered the halls of Valhalla, his eyes were sad and his countenance dark. The first one he encountered was Odhr. Odhr was surprised at Odin's demeanor and asked: "Odin, what did you see on the earth that has disturbed you so?"

Odin answered: "Oh, the human race is in a bad way! They are becoming more and more forgetful of the world of light. Many have become two-faced, jealous, and bickering. When they sleep at night the dark spirits sprinkle hate and greed into their souls. They lust after gold and earthly treasures. The works of the gods that are illumined by the sun get little attention, and many people have become blind to their beauty."

While Odin was speaking, Freya, Odhr's beautiful wife, came up to them. She said: "Odhr, sing a new song so that Odin can forget his troubles." Odhr began to sing a song about the sun and the glittering dew in the early morning and the opening of countless thousands of flower buds. He sang of the first shimmer of light on the ocean at sunrise to the last glimmer of evening light on the mountains and clouds. His song brought the other gods to listen. As it was ending, the hall was filled with listeners. The last note resounded. A blessed stillness lay over Valhalla.

Odin walked up to Odhr. His countenance was bright and cheerful. He said to the singer: "Dear Odhr, your song has shown me how the human race can be saved from the evil, hateful beings of Hel. Do not delay! Take the Rainbow Bridge, to Midgard! Sing your songs to the people and they will be healed and their souls will become healthy again."

When Freya heard Odin's words she was very taken aback. She did not want to see her husband, Odhr, go away. She worried that he may not be able to get back. She said: "Odin, please do not send him away from Valhalla! He is so innocent and good. He knows neither evil nor deceit as both have been brought to the humans by the bad spirits of Schwarzalfaheim. He may be harmed by the evil spirits of darkness."

Odin looked at Odhr. Odhr lifted his head and answered: "Freya, what Odin has suggested is good! Yes, I will go to the people and bring them songs. I will teach them to sing so that they learn through words and sounds that the beautiful earth is but a reflection of heaven and will so honor it once again." After these words Odin blessed the courageous singer.

But Freya was very concerned. She had a dark premonition that she might lose Odhr. But Odhr went via the Rainbow Bridge to the earth and the people. He took on a human form. He appeared to people in a white robe and sang his songs to them.

And so it happened that wherever his voice could be heard, people gathered in large numbers! They listened joyfully to the sounds and the divine words. Cold hearts were warmed. Crumpled souls unfolded once again. Closed eyes were opened again and looked in awe at the beauty of nature. Odhr sang songs about the lightning and thunder of a storm and the colorful glow of a rainbow. He sang about all the things that the sun made beautiful upon the earth.

The tone of Odhr's voice penetrated the hearts of the people so that many eyes filled with tears. The tears washed the poison out of their souls. When night fell, no one went to bed while Odhr sang the song of the night. It was about the moon and the stars and the eternal gods who lived in the light even when darkness covered the earth. Listening shyly at first but then with more vigor, the people hummed and sang along with Odhr.

Odhr was very happy when he heard his melodies echoing to him from the people. When that happened he would move on to another area. Once the people learned how to sing, hate and bitterness were soon forgotten. The people sang about the works of creation and honored the gods who had created the world.

Odhr sang the song of planting and harvest. He sang the songs of the fishermen, shepherds, blacksmiths, and spinners. The songs became more and more rooted in the people. When Odhr finished his work and returned to Valhalla, he left behind singing people upon the earth. Odin took him into his heart with much joy.

But the evil spirits of the deep were not happy. Those in Schwarzalfaheim were angry because they could no longer get to human souls while they slept. They thought about other ways to tear the people away from heaven. Odin was aware of this.

Time marched on. The first time the ravens returned from earth with a report about the terrible things happening there, Odin spoke to Odhr: "Noble singer! Your songs have done much good on the earth, but your work is only half finished. Prepare for a second journey. You shall go to Schwarzalfaheim, into the dark kingdom. Your songs must be taken to the root of the problem. Your singing may bring the evil spirits back into their home of light which they have abandoned to live in the dark depths. The magic of your songs will bring them strength to change back to the good!"

Odhr thought this over for a long time. Finally he answered: "My heart says yes! I want to do it!" His wife, Freya, did not know to where he was traveling when he bid her farewell.

On hidden paths and through dark tunnels Odhr made his way to the gates of the kingdom of darkness. The demonic residents were whirling around like bats. Nobody stood in his way or tried to bar him from entering. He took a deep breath and went inside singing. He walked through dim, narrow corridors.

The further he went the harder it was to breathe in the deathly close air. His singing evoked screeching, howling, and whistling out of the crevices. He paid no attention and sang on as strongly as he could. That silenced many of the spirits and they began to listen. He sang about things they had never heard of before. Many frowning faces relaxed into smooth countenances. Some of them followed behind Odhr and moved in time to the music. The procession got nearer to the large hall of Schwarzalfaheim where the king of darkness lived.

A flying messenger had already warned the king and so he had prepared a cup of the most horrible poison. He said to the messenger: "When the singer enters the Dark Hall give him this drink as a welcome. Pretend to be friendly. Say clever things!"

The messenger stood by the entrance and waited. In the glowing firelight he saw the singer coming closer surrounded by dancing spirits. The messenger stepped forward with the cup in his hand and made a sign of welcome. Odhr stopped. The cup bearer said: "Divine brother, I offer you this welcome drink in the name of our king. Take the refreshment and sing us a song about Asgard and Valhalla!" Odhr was very happy that someone from Schwarzalfaheim was so friendly. He took the cup and drank.

In that instant the poison made him fall to the ground. One of the evil ones immediately ripped open an artery with his sharp tooth. A third one brought a kettle and let Odhr's blood flow into it. All life left his body.

Odhr never returned to Valhalla. His divine soul sank into the foundations of the world. The evil ones of Schwarzalfaheim were jubilant. The king praised them and said: "Bury the kettle in the deepest crevice so that the singer's blood may never get into the hands of the gods."

A long time passed and still Odhr did not return to Valhalla. Freya cried golden tears. Odin was very worried. He sent one of the ravens to the entrance of Schwarzalfaheim at night to listen. Soon the raven returned with a report: "I heard two spirits of darkness talking to each other. This is what they said: 'Since Odhr drank from the cup and we buried his blood in the kettle, we must always stand guard at the entrance so that nobody comes in unnoticed. It's about time someone was relieving us of this guard duty!' "

When Odin heard this, he knew for certain that Odhr was dead. He fell into deep mourning. No more singing was to be heard in Valhalla. Freya was inconsolable. In his pain, Odin had a thought: "We must retrieve the singer's blood and return it to Valhalla!"

Now, Odin had the ability to change himself into other forms. He started out on his journey and at the entrance to Schwarzalfaheim transformed himself into a snake. He slithered through the corridors and caves until he found the hidden kettle. Odin spread a magic luminescence around himself as he carried the kettle out so that nobody could see him. Once outside Odin unfolded his wings. He took the container with its precious contents back to Asgard.

At the Rainbow Bridge, there was a guard named Heimdall. It was his duty to give every human soul on its way to an earth life a drink from the Cup of Forgetfulness. That way it could forget everything that had happened before and begin a new life as a child.

Odin sought out Heimdall and spoke to him: "I give you a cup with the blood of the singer, Odhr. Every so often you shall put a drop of this blood into a human soul so that person will become a singer, storyteller, or poet." Heimdall did as he was told. Since that time there are people born again and again in Midgard who love to sing and compose. That is how the art of Odhr began to bloom in thousands of people. And, the Schwarzalfaheim spirits still have trouble getting close to a singing soul.

That was the end of Evart's story in German's new house. The only thing to be heard was the crackling of the fire. Hoegge was slumbering at Evart's feet.

The soft voice of Helga broke the silence: "Evart, please, sing us a lullaby! One can fall asleep easily with some of Odhr's music." The Druid began to sing a tender song. He sang about how Freya's tears turned into precious gems in the earth. Other tears became little stars in the night sky. They shine down at night and create the flowers' perfume. It was a long, sleepy song.

When it was over Evart took Hoegge in his arms and carried him to a pile of straw where he would sleep. He covered the coals with ashes so they would not burn out during the night. Then he sought his own bed of straw. As he was falling asleep he heard someone singing softly. It was Helga. Evart thought: "It's good. She's singing in her sleep. She got a drop of Odhr's blood."

Once in the night someone cried out. It was Hoegge. He was fighting: "You rotten demon! Just wait, I'll get you!" A fist was pounded into the straw and then all was silent once again.

The Procession

The Druid was the first to arise in the dawn light and go outside. Uralda was taking care of the hearth fire. She blew into the ashes and murmured her fire verse. Soon the flames were going again. There was a rustling of straw from all sides. Holding declared upon awakening: "Holger, Helga, Hoegge, we're riding back home early today. After you've had a drink of milk we'll start."

Holger replied: "Father, let us stay here. Evart wants to make a procession this morning with the ashes from yesterday's sacrifice. He will spread them on the fields to bless them for the winter. I would like to participate and help him."

Holder's wife, Hulda, agreed with her son: "Druid Evart told me he would teach the children this afternoon about mushrooms and herbs found in the forest. That will surely take until sundown. Evart is also staying the night one more time. Holding, let the children stay until tomorrow. They will surely learn good and useful things!" Helga gave her mother a joyful hug.

Holding agreed under one condition: "Then Mother will ride home on Holger's horse and you three can come home tomorrow on foot." Soon after sunrise the Holding parents rode back home.

Hoegge said: "When Father is not here life is a lot more fun." And he did a somersault.

At the place of sacrifice in front of the house, Geron and Holger used a small wooden shovel to put the cold ashes into a basket. Evart and the others gathered there. Evart said: "When we start out to the fields, Geron and Holger will walk in front with the basket. Ina will carry an armful of grain stalks as fruit of the field. Uralda will bring dried balderbrau along to toss onto the field at intervals. German and Gerwin shall drive the milk cow. Gerda will bring apples as fruit of the trees, and Helga shall carry sheep's wool. Hoegge will carry the water jug for me. Go now and prepare everything. Then we will begin."

In a little while everything was ready for the procession and Evart gave the signal to begin. He walked toward the fields that had already been harvested. Only the winter planting was showing its green sprouts. The Druid spread ashes on the field with a shovel and thanked the root spirits of the earth. As he tossed a second shovelful to the ground he thanked the water spirits in the rain and dew. He sprinkled water from Hoegge's jug using a pine branch. The third time he threw the ashes high into the air and thanked the spirits of the air that brought growth to all the leaves. The fourth time he threw the ashes as high into the air as he could. He thanked the spirits of light and warmth which allowed the grain and fruit to ripen.

And so it went from field to field until the ash basket was empty. Nobody spoke during all of this. Even Hoegge was good. Of course, Evart was holding his hand. The procession ended when the cow lay down in the field. Everyone stood in a circle around the cow. Evart to sing a simple earth-blessing song that had only one verse repeated over and over:

> Mother earth, we thank you,
> Heavenly Father, we praise you.
> Thank you for fruit, for milk, and cattle!
> Plants, animals, grain, and food,
> Give us strength for our earthly journey.

They all sang this verse as they walked a circle around the cow, six times to the right for the half-year that the sun was on the rise and six times to the left for the half-year that the sun was sinking. Hoegge thought it was a little boring. He began to hop and skip and sometimes did one of his sweet somersaults which did not really bother anyone.

The children were allowed to pick the last of the autumn flowers and arrange them around the cow's horns by sticking them in the rope halter. Hoegge braided his flowers into the hair on the cow's tail. Then the finely decorated cow was brought back to the rest of the grazing herd, and the fruit and grain that had been blessed was taken back to the house. Evart said: "Fasten them to a door post. It will be food for the birds in the winter."

In Forest and Meadow

The children needed to do some chores around the house such as wood chopping and cleaning. When they were finished Evart said to Ina: "Get three baskets that we can take into the forest; one for mushrooms, one for beechnuts, and the third for acorns."

German said: "I can't do without Geron today. Holding left his ax here just for today so we have to make good use of it. We must still chop a lot of wood for the winter from the felled trees."

So Evart went with the boys and girls into the forest. Helga and Gerda carried the two smaller baskets and Gerwin and Holger the larger one for the mushrooms. Hoegge wanted to sit in the large basket so he jumped right in. Gerwin and Holger began to swing the basket back and forth until Hoegge screamed as much from fear as happiness and Waldo came up barking excitedly. The boys started swinging the basket faster and higher. When they ran by Evart he said, laughing: "Just keep it up! Hoegge needs lots of exercise!"

Finally they became too tired to continue and set the basket on the ground. Hoegge crawled out on all fours with the basket on his head. He was still in the mood for play and grunted like a wild boar. Waldo hunted him down and sprang onto Hoegge's back, fell off, and barked wildly, which in turn made Hoegge all the wilder. He did not notice that he was running toward a very large rock. Helga screamed: "Watch out, Hoegge!" But Hoegge could not hear her for the barking. Hoegge was running like a wild steer and he hit the rock head first. He lay there stunned for a moment. Then he crawled out from under the basket. He covered his bleeding nose with both hands but he did not cry. The onlookers did not know whether to laugh or offer help. Hoegge wiped his bloody hands on the grass.

Evart found a healing herb growing near the rock and he put it into Hoegge's nose to stop the bleeding. Evart told Hoegge: "Just lie down there for a bit. The yarrow will soon stop the bleeding. Breathe through your mouth for awhile."

Evart sat on the big rock and waved the others over to sit on the grass in front of him. He had used his knife to dig a plant out of the ground with its roots. He held up the plant and explained: "In order for the plant to grow, it requires four things: earth, water, air, and warm light. Under the earth are the root gnomes. They give the roots little beards. Fat gnomes make the carrot roots. The water spirits dance in the water. They form the leaves out of the watery juice in the plants. The spirits of the air weave delicate forms and change the leaves into flowers at the top. The elves of light work their secretive magic in every flower bud. They bring the energy from the sun, moon, and stars into the flowers. That is why the flowers have forms that resemble the sun, moon, and stars. When the buds open they receive the energy of the fire spirits from the sun's warmth. They put perfume and honey into the flowers. They fly with the bees and butterflies all around and make the fruit ripen. They form the new seeds and give them such strong, fiery life energy that the seed does not lose its life force throughout the whole winter."

Gerda asked: "Why don't we see the gnomes and the elves? Can we never see them?"

The Druid smiled and said: "Normal human eyes have become dull. When one goes often into nature and really concentrates on a flower, one can sometimes see them. The gnomes are the easiest to see. Holger has seen them."

Helga added: "Yes, and a short time ago he saw some elves in the evening light. He told me."

Suddenly Hoegge spoke: "Father Evart, can you see them?"

Evart replied: "Yes, Hoegge, I see them. In the Druid school one learns to see the invisible beings with one's inner eyes. Just before, when you ran into this rock, two little gnomes came out and laughed. The gnomes think that much of what people do is funny or stupid.

Then they grin from ear to ear. But when you were lying on the ground with a bloody nose, one of the gnomes pointed to the little herb plant that I put in your nose. But, come now, we want to gather mushrooms, beechnuts, and acorns so we have something good to take back home."

Hoegge asked: "Are the two gnomes still here?"

Evart pointed to a nearby oak tree and said: "There where the roots go into the ground they are sitting and looking out at us with curiosity. Gnomes love human children, and the youngest children are the ones they love best."

Hoegge nodded with satisfaction. He stood up and said: "My nose has stopped bleeding, but I'll leave the gnome herbs in for now."

They put the baskets down in a forest clearing and began the search for mushrooms. Evart described three varieties: edible, inedible, and poisonous. Gerwin went with Holger who knew almost every sort of mushroom because he had often accompanied Evart on mushroom expeditions. The girls and Hoegge went with Evart. The basket was getting full.

All at once Hoegge came into the clearing jumping for joy. In each hand he was holding a bright red mushroom with white spots on it. He shouted: "Here is the most beautiful and surely the best mushroom to eat in the world! I'd like to bite into it right now and eat it raw."

Evart grabbed Hoegge's wrist and said: "Stop! They are extremely poisonous. They would very painfully press the life out of you in a very short time. Those are the most poisonous mushrooms of all! Throw them away. Go to the stream and wash your hands well. Their poison can stick to the skin." Hoegge threw his find as hard as he could, hurried to the nearby stream and washed his hands with mud, sand, and water until they were as red as the mushroom.

When the large basket was filled with good mushrooms Evart said: "Uralda will make a wonderful mushroom soup tonight. We will spread out the others by the fire to dry. They will make good winter provision."

Now they were ready to gather beechnuts and acorns. Evart taught them: "The fat beechnuts are good, but sometimes there are smaller, misshapen ones that are empty or have a wormhole and have been eaten away." The ground under many of the beech trees was covered with beechnuts. With twelve hands working, the basket was soon filled to the brim.

Hoegge could not resist biting into some of the nuts now and again, but nobody thought of curbing his joy in this activity. Once he went up to Evart and declared: "I cannot chew or swallow right when my nose is stopped up. Can I take the gnome herbs out now?" Evart carefully removed the packing from Hoegge's nose and it was better again. It even occurred to Hoegge, although a little later, to thank Evart for his help.

From a short distance away one of the girls suddenly gave a scream. It was Helga and she came running with flying hair to Evart and shouted: "A bear! A horrible bear!" She clung to Evart and was shaking uncontrollably. Everyone ran to Evart. Hoegge crawled between his legs to hide.

Evart stood fast and looked in the direction from which Helga had come running. He ordered: "Stay still! Nobody move! Nothing will happen to you."

A noise that sounded like breaking branches could be heard. A powerful brown bear appeared from out of the bushes nearby. He raised his head, stood still, sniffed the air, and gazed toward the mushroom gatherers. Evart whispered: "Walk slowly backwards behind the big beech tree."

Gerwin held tight to Waldo who was shaking all over but made no sound. Holger had noticed that Evart was a little pale and his eyes had become glassy. The Druid loosened Helga's hands from his arm and said: "Holger, take them all back!" Then Evart slowly walked forward, step by step, toward the bear. The children went with Waldo behind the beech tree. The bear's head was restlessly turning from side to side as it sniffed the air again and then let out a deep growl. The children listened.

Evart began to speak to the bear. Holger peeked nervously around the tree trunk to watch Evart and the brown bear. At first the Druid's words were gentle and friendly in tone. The closer he came to the bear, the more commanding his tone became. He made a sign in the air and shouted a strong word that Holger did not understand. The bear began to rock back and forth as if confused as to what it should do. Evart continued talking and walked closer. Slowly, the bear began to step backwards. Suddenly he turned and walked back into the bushes.

The Druid stood still for awhile and then walked slowly back to the children. He was quite pale. Sweat was on his brow from the enormous effort. He said abruptly: "Get the baskets, we're going home!"

Nobody said a word. They all hurried. From time to time Evart would look behind them, but the bear was nowhere in sight. As they reached the edge of the forest Hoegge said: "Now I know what to do with a bear. Walk up to it and scream at it!"

That evening they were all sitting around the fire sipping mushroom soup. Hoegge asked: "Evart, where would I be now if the poisonous mushroom had killed me?"

Evart pointed to the burning coals and answered: "Just as bright flames and dark smoke go out of the wood, so do our brightly shining souls leave our bodies when we die. But they always take a little bit of the dark soul-smoke with them. They travel to the land of the dead. There they must clean away the soul smoke. Then they can go on into the land of the stars. There the souls go on a long journey."

Hoegge asked: "Do we still have feet to walk?"

Evart answered: "Souls that have died are more like the birds and can fly."

Hoegge said: "Nice. I always wanted to fly." He ate some more of the good mushroom soup. But suddenly he had another question: "And after that, do we come back to earth?"

Evart laughed and said: "Yes, you also have come down on the Rainbow Bridge and drunk from the Cup of Forgetfulness." The fire crackled. Evart spoke again: "A little fire gnome was very happy that Hoegge got an answer to his question."

German was very concerned that a brown bear had come into the forest making it unsafe for his family. There had not been a bear around for a very long time. Normally one had to ride very far away to go on a bear hunt.

That is why German said to Geron: "Tomorrow the two of us will try to get that bear. We should examine the bows and arrows before bedtime and sharpen the knives." Some of the arrows were made from hard wood and needed to be sharpened. Four arrows had valuable iron points that had to be rubbed with fat from time to time. The bows also had to be oiled and tested to make sure they could still hold up under the strongest pressure. Two wooden lances with iron tips and two daggers were also made ready. German asked his oldest son: "Shall we ask Wugo to accompany us on the hunt? He has a lot of experience with bears."

Geron answered: "No, Father, I'd rather not. You know how much I practiced shooting my bow and arrow this summer, and Wugo would probably want half of the kill even though we are three people." German did not mind and so they agreed to go with just the two of them.

The Druid Tells the Story of Baldur

While German and Geron were busy looking after the hunting weapons, all the others sat around the hearth fire. Gerwin and Holger were cutting up mushrooms into narrow strips. Hoegge was overseeing the fire so that it gave good light. Ina, Uralda, and the girls were stringing the strips of mushrooms to hang them up to dry. Evart was silently staring into space. Gerwin asked him: "Evart, would you tell us another story about the gods? Is there one that tells about weapons?"

The Druid answered: "Yes, I can tell you a story about arrows and spears."

There was a time when the gods of Valhalla could enjoy the brilliant, radiating light of the god Baldur. His robe was woven from sun rays. When the evil spirits and demons of Schwarzalfaheim awakened bad, dark thoughts in human beings, Baldur would bring them light into their nights and good dreams. That way they could begin their days with a bright outlook. The kingdom of the gnomes and elves was revealed underground and also in the trees and flowers. This made the souls of people grateful and pious.

But another time was nearing. Frigga, Baldur's mother, had dark dreams that told her the Kingdom of Darkness would do some harm to Baldur. The gods became worried about him. Frigga wandered through all the worlds to reassure herself that no being wanted to harm her son. Even the giants said: 'Sun warm, sun good! We do not want to harm Baldur!' The trees, plants, and animals also gave their word that they would not do anything to hurt Baldur.

Odin, however, rode on his heavenly steed, Sleipnir, to Niflheim in order to consult with the seer Wala. He wanted to ask her if anything was threatening Baldur. She awakened out of her sleep and said: 'Baldur will die. His spirit will leave Valhalla and move out into the wide world.'

Odin returned to Valhalla to find the gods occupied with an amusing game on the heavenly meadow. Baldur stood cheerfully in the middle. They were throwing spears and arrows at him, but nothing could hit him and do him any injury.

The troublemaking god, Loki, came creeping up. He was also often seen in the Dark Worlds. What he saw angered him because he could not stand to be in the presence of Baldur's pure light. He made himself appear as a woman, walked up to Frigga, and asked her: 'Have you made sure that all the living things will do no harm to Baldur?'

Frigga answered: 'Yes, I have; except a little tiny plant east of Valhalla with white berries, high up on a tree. It seemed to be so young and harmless that I did not bother it.'

That is exactly what Loki wanted to find out. He quickly flew off and soon found the mistletoe plant on top of a tree. He fashioned an arrow out of the woody stem and returned to Baldur's meadow. The old and blind god, Hoedur, was standing there. Loki said to him: 'Here, I have brought you a bow and arrow so that you may also shoot with your powerful strength. You string the bow and I will aim it for you toward Baldur.' Hoedur pulled back the bowstring and let fly the arrow that Loki had aimed at Baldur.

A cry of pain resounded and Baldur sank to the ground. His spirit left his body and he was never again to sit at the gods' table. On the earth, people's dreams became darker.

Fewer and fewer people gazed at the light of the flowers and the stars. The weaving of the elves and the work of the gnomes became hidden to people. Their eyes became dim. Even in the world of the gods it had become darker.

Evart the Druid was silent. Suddenly Hoegge spoke up: "Can one not bring back Baldur? Can the gods not free him from Helheim?"

The question surprised Evart. He thought for awhile before answering: "It is our hope that someday he will return. Perhaps he is even now on his star journey."

Holger asked: "Will he go back to the sun?"

Evart answered: "The prophecy is that he will come to the earth and reside here. In what form, we still do not know. But now, today was long, let us get some rest. Tomorrow will be a hard day for our bear hunters."

The Bear Hunt

Very early in the morning father and son started off on their hunt in the forest. On his way out Geron grabbed the ax that was hanging by the door and stuck it in his belt. Evart would be returning home that morning with Holding's children. German picked up a handful of dry leaves as they entered the forest and threw it into the air. Then he observed which way the wind carried them. He said: "It is good. The wind is coming against us. We can go with confidence. I think the bear must have gone into the deeper part of the forest for the night. From now on we will walk with about fifty paces apart so that we have a wider field of vision. A single cuckoo call will be our signal. Repetition of the signal will mean you have found something. In that case, we must quickly get closer together again. May Tyr strengthen us!"

They parted the fifty paces. Geron walked noiselessly on the mossy forest floor; every muscle and nerve ready to spring into action. In his left hand he held the bow with an arrow ready to shoot, and in his right hand he held the lance. From time to time he would stand still and listen intently.

The two hunters went deeper and deeper into the forest. Suddenly Geron heard the double signal. He hurried to his father's side, making as little noise as possible. German was standing next to a bush but he had no weapon raised. He pointed to the mossy ground and whispered: "This is where the bear spent the night. Moss, leaves, and plants are pressed flat."

They discovered a hunk of fur stuck to a nearby tree trunk. German said: "Here is where he rubbed his back." Further searching revealed the direction the bear must have gone. Broken ferns showed the bear's path. German said: "Let us stay close together. His sleeping place is still slightly warm. He can't have been gone from here very long." Geron put the palm of his hand where the bear had slept. When one pressed on the moss one could still feel a little of the bear's warmth.

The two hunters continued walking very slowly and carefully without leaving each other's sight. Geron's blood was hammering in his veins so hard that he could feel it in his neck.

Suddenly, not fifty feet away, two birds flew up screeching. Geron stood still. A crackle! Leaves and branches moved. It must be the bear. Geron whistled the double cuckoo call as a signal. The animal broke through the bushes and raised his head. Geron took cover behind a tree trunk.

German was coming toward him from the side, but a small tree was blocking his view of the bear. Geron pointed in the direction of his discovery. German went quietly from tree to tree, coming ever closer. When he had almost reached Geron, the bear must have seen a movement. The powerful beast let out a low growl. He scratched a tree with his claws as if trying to sharpen them.

German finally reached Geron and whispered: "Just a little closer and then we shoot the first arrows!" They separated again and every few steps hid behind trees. Geron was nervous and he shot the first arrow, but it was too high and flew right over the bear. Then German's arrow could be heard. It hit the the bear's hind leg.

The bear roared angrily, bit the arrow, and was able to get it out. But now he looked around for his attacker and he was fighting mad. He trotted back and forth, raising his snout into the air. Geron's second arrow hit the bear in the shoulder, but the bone stopped the arrow from going any deeper. When German stepped into the open to get a better shot, the bear saw him. The arrow hit the bear in the throat. He sprang towards his attacker. Geron let loose his third arrow. German quickly grabbed the spear lying on the ground. He could not afford to miss the bear this time because he would not get another chance.

The bear leaped at German, but his spear only glanced off the bear's fur. Geron hurried to assist his father. German had drawn his knife, but the blade of a knife was not sufficient to stop an angry bear. A well-aimed thrust caused the bear to fall to the ground. At that moment Geron thrust his lance into the beast's back. Geron tore the ax from his belt and was able to give the bear a death blow on its skull.

Now Geron turned his full attention to his father. He had a deep wound on his shoulder, bleeding badly. Geron tore off a piece of the already torn jacket and pressed it to the wound. Then he loosened his father's belt and wrapped it tightly around his shoulder and upper arm. The wounded man moaned and was barely conscious.

Geron could see that the bear was no longer moving. He knelt down: "Father, I'm going for help. I'll be right back. Maybe Evart is still nearby!" His father nodded. He had understood.

Now Geron ran through the forest as he had never run before. Once out of the forest he drank some water from the stream and washed his bloody arm. He had also been clawed by the bear. Gerda was watching the sheep on the meadow. She was shocked when she saw Geron stumbling toward her. He called: "Is Evart still here? Father is badly injured!"

Gerda answered: "He just left with the Holdings. He's walking. The children are sitting on his horse. He cannot have gotten far."

Geron ran to the house. Ina, Uralda, and Gerwin were in a nearby field harvesting carrots. He hurried to them and shouted: "Father is injured in the forest. The bear is dead. Get herbs and water ready. I'm going with the horse to get Evart." He ran to the stable, jumped on his horse and galloped away.

Geron soon caught up to Evart and the children. He and Holger were walking while Helga and Hoegge sat on his horse. "Evart, will you come with me to Father in the forest? The bear injured him. His shoulder is bleeding very badly. Please, save his life!"

Evart thought for just a moment and then said: "Children, get down from the horse and walk back to the house. I will ride with Geron to his father." The Druid mounted his horse and both rode off to German. They stopped at the house on their way. Evart got some clean linen from Uralda; also some herbs and a jug of water with a lid. They continued. Geron knew that his father must get help very soon or he would bleed to death.

When they arrived where German lay on the ground he was still conscious. Evart could tell by the weakness of the wounded man that already much life had flowed out of him. He knelt down and pressed both hands on the wound without loosening Geron's bandage. He began murmuring strange words. Geron knew that it was blood magic. Now, Evert gave German to drink out of the jug until it was empty. Geron could hear how Evart was talking in a sing-song fashion. He observed how his father then went to sleep. Finally Evart turned to Geron: "You need to take care of the bear now. Get your people to help you. I will stay here with your father. He may not be moved yet."

Geron asked: "Will Father live?"

The Druid nodded: "Yes, I hope that he comes through. Take the jug back with you and bring more water. German must drink lots of water. Put a little honey in it."

So Geron rode back and was able to give them some hope by telling them that Evart was optimistic. Knives and baskets were hurriedly made ready. Ina prepared honey water for German. The sheep were brought back to the stable. With the two horses, everyone except Uralda returned to the forest to butcher the bear and bring the meat back to the house. It would have been impossible to bring the animal whole back to the house.

Once back in the forest Evart warned everyone to stay very quiet. He said to Ina: "German is sleeping. Sleep is precious now." Ina held back her tears. Evart's presence gave her hope and courage.

Everyone was amazed at the powerful bear! But, of course, their happiness was dampened by German's condition. Ina, Geron, and Gerwin began to cut away the fur. Evart suggested: "Gerwin and Gerda, cut down four thin, straight and small trees. Cut off the branches. We will build a litter for your father to carry him home." They both got to work right away. Evart searched out fresh herbs and cut linen into wide strips. Everything was now ready to further treat the wound when German awoke. Evart helped Geron to skin the bear.

German awoke. He was thirsty again. He drank half the honey water at one go. Evart asked if German could move his finger. Yes, that was good. Could he raise his lower arm? That was also good. But when he tried to raise his whole arm he gritted his teeth in pain. It was impossible.

Evart carefully removed the cloth that Geron had bound around the wound. The wound was now visible. Ina helped Evart to lay on the herbs and bandage the wound again with the linen strips. She let Geron finish the butchering alone. Geron had often helped his father with the butchering of large animals, once even an ox. But a bear rendered much more meat than that and it must all be done and ready to carry home before nightfall. Otherwise, the wild animals would take it.

Evart had made a sling for German's arm out of his leather belt. German asked in a dull voice: "Will I be able to use my arm again?"

The Druid replied: "Nothing is broken and the fingers are fine. But the muscle has been badly torn. If the wound fever is not too bad then everything may turn out all right. But the moon will be full a few more times before you have any strength in the arm. You must learn to have a lot of patience, German. Every piece of bad luck has its purpose."

Evart spoke to Ina: "The third day will be the worst. The fever will practically burn him up. I will stay with you until it is over." Ina thankfully took Evart's hand and mumbled some words of thanks.

Then Evart did something strange. He put the bearskin on the ground with the fur side facing down and said: "German, we are going to lay you inside this fresh, damp bearskin and wrap it around you. It will strengthen your life force."

German was able to stand with Evart's help and lay down upon the skin which was really quite bloody in places. The Druid said: "Bear blood is also a medicine."

Gerwin and Gerda had returned with the wood for the litter. Gerda asked: "What have you done with Father?"

Ina pointed to the bearskin from which a bit of German's beard could be seen poking through. She explained: "The bearskin will keep him warm and give him strength."

Evart told Gerwin: "Get on the horse. Take the jug and go milk a cow for your father. Tell Uralda that we have good hope for your father, but come right back with the milk."

Gerwin looked over at Geron. Geron said: "Take Father's horse! Bring some burning coals in a clay jug and also some pieces of leather."

Geron had separated the bear meat into various piles. It was a good thing that the ax was there so that he could chop through the bones with it. Ina helped him with everything. She gathered all the fat and lay it in a special pile.

Evart and Gerda made two litters, one for German and one for the meat. Evart said to Geron: "Bring me the bone from one of the bear's front legs!" The Druid split the bone with the ax. Then he carefully cut out the marrow with a knife. He took it to German who had been watching Ina and Geron at work and occasionally giving them advice.

Evart said: "Here, German, eat this marrow, as much as you can. It will help to build new blood!" He put the marrow beside German where he could take it with his good arm.

Gerwin returned with milk and hot coals. He had put several pieces of leather underneath him as a saddle. Geron wanted to lay them on top of the litter to carry the meat. Father drank the milk in large gulps. Geron told Gerwin to make a fire and to roast some of the meat for their dinner.

Slowly the mood lightened. Everyone had been so worried about German, but now things looked much better. Gerda went to sit by Gerwin. Soon there was a crackling fire going. Gerwin and his sister were able to build a spit using a few pieces of wood. Evart used some lengths of bear intestines to strengthen the litter, tying it up like with string. Ina sighed: "Where can we store all of this meat?"

The answer came from inside the bearskin: "We'll hang it from the rafters in the old house and smoke it."

Gerwin called everyone to eat. Geron brought his father some meat from a front paw and said: "Now you can eat the paw that nearly killed you!"

Father smiled for the first time that evening. He said: "And Gerda can make you a necklace from the claws and teeth, you bear killer!"

While eating, the group discussed how they would transport German home. Evart suggested: "Gerwin should stay here with the weapons and the meat. Keep the fire going so that wild animals like fox and weasel can't get to the meat. Gerda can lead both horses by the reins. We will load them up with bear hocks. Geron will carry the litter in front and Ina and I will carry it in back."

German said: "I'm so sorry you have to carry me. I would rather walk or ride."

Evart said quickly: "Not a chance! The wound might reopen and bleed more. That would be serious!" So German had to give in. All five people pulled and lifted until German was situated on the litter. So everything turned out for the best, just as Evart said it would.

The World Ash Tree – Yggdrasil

Night had fallen before all the bear meat had been carried home. The wounded German had a high fever. He was lying on a straw bed in the new house. Evart cared for him which was a comfort to everyone after the shocking events of the day. All hands were busy hanging the bear meat in the old house to be smoked. There was a fire that was fed green wood and that produced a lot of smoke. It would preserve the meat for the winter. Uralda was using the three-legged pan to melt bear fat. She poured it into a big clay pot. That would also be winter provision.

Late in the evening they all gathered around the hearth in the new house. German was in a deep, feverish sleep. Evart seemed satisfied and said: "We will let him lie in the bearskin until tomorrow morning. Then, however, the skin has to be rubbed with wood ash and oak bark so that it becomes real leather." Strange as it seems, nobody was interested in sleeping even though they were all exhausted.

Gerda asked: "Evart, how is it with the soul that lives in the body?"

Evart answered: "I will tell you a story about the ash tree world known as Yggdrasil. There is a lot about the human soul in that story. You see, people and the world are one. People are like trees between heaven and earth, but they can walk around."

Once upon a time the gods created a tree that was a world unto itself. It was an ash tree. The human soul was modeled after this tree. This ash tree had three roots, a strong trunk, and an impressive crown of branches that reached far out toward the sun, moon, and stars. An eagle sat at the very top of the tree. It had a view of the world and flew over it just like we do with our thoughts. A little hawk sat on the eagle's beak, and it could observe exactly what was going on in the world just like we can with our eyes.

Four elk lived in the crown of the tree and munched the leaves. Their antlers caught the heavenly light from overhead day and night. The elk were able to transform the light into dewdrops that would fall from their antlers and bring good things to the world: the nightly dew for the plants and the nectar perfume for the flowers and bees. People still receive refreshing dew for their souls during the night when they sleep so that they will be cheerful in the morning.

However, under one of the three roots there lives a dark dragon. His name is Nydhoegger. He gets angry when the good dewdrops fall to earth and make their way to the people. He shouts: 'Awful dew! It burns me! If only I could climb up there and bite the elk and chase away the eagle!'

But whenever Nydhoegger becomes angry like that, the squirrel Ratatoeskr, who is very curious, comes and listens. It quickly springs up the tree to the elk and the eagle. It tells them what the dragon says about them and how he has threatened them.

The eagle says: 'Nydhoegger does not know the sun. He is fighting from a position of darkness.'

But the elk say: 'If he would eat a little less of the root, we would have more leaves to eat.' Then Ratatoeskr scrambles back down the tree and tells the dragon everything he has heard up above. The dragon only gets angry again and grumbles. But he is unable to stop the elk dew from dripping down to the earth.

A fountain is located by the second root. It gathers the water of life. That way the tree cannot die. But Nydhoegger and the evil ones in the dark world wish that the tree would die along with the whole creation of the gods.

The third root is in the middle and it goes into the human realm, into the human heart. The three Norns live there at the fountain of birth and death. They spin the life threads of people. Some people get long threads and some get short threads, depending on what is right for each person. The Norns are very wise. Urd looks back into the past and knows from whence the human souls come. Verdandi sees the present, and Skuld looks into the future where everything is in a state of becoming. She knows that every person makes mistakes and must suffer the consequences. But she also knows that a new life can allow a person to make improvements.

So the three Norns spin the life thread into our hearts, the past, present, and future. When a person dies they sever the thread of destiny. Then the soul gets to drink from the fountain that contains the water of life. That way it can get by Nydhoegger unharmed because only the body dies; the soul lives on.

Evart put another stick of wood onto the fire. Gerda asked: "Evart, what happens to the soul when the body is given back to the earth?"

Evart answered: "It travels over the Rainbow Bridge and on hidden paths back into Heaven. Later it can find its way back to a new life on earth. As many people as die will be reborn."

Gerwin asked: "Evart, you have told us about the fountain near the root. What kind of water is it?"

Evart answered: "It is Mimir's fountain. An eye of the god Odin is resting on the clear bottom. He sacrificed an eye so that human speech could come out of the fountain. The ability to speak and think are gifts from the gods. The animals cannot do that. For this reason we humans should always address each other with human speech and not bark, caw, growl, or grunt!"

Everyone chuckled. The Druid said: "Let us go to sleep now. We will get the elk dew and be fresh for the new day. And may Yggdrasil give your father healing strength from the water of life!"

Uralda and Ina thanked Evart for telling the children some of the secrets of life.

The cheerful laughter awakened German. Geron helped Evart to make some herb tea for German and place his arm in a more comfortable position. When everyone was lying on their straw beds, Geron whispered to Evart who was sleeping nearby: "Evart, do only people from Germany have Norns who watch over their souls? How is it with the Romans?"

Evart answered quietly: "Every human being has a protecting spirit, even the Romans. They call their goddesses of destiny "The Three Fates."

Geron went on: "What happens with a slave like Virtus, the Roman? Wugo tortures him and whips him for very small offenses."

The Druid answered: "The Norns may let a person sink into misery for a time so that he is humbled and can bring himself up again out of his own strength, or perhaps with the help of a friend."

Geron was silent and thought about these words. The help of a friend? Virtus had become his friend in some small way, had he not, since he felt sorry for him? For the first time he had the little flicker of the thought: "Virtus must be free. I could help him!"

On the fourth day after the bear attack, Evart could start his journey home. German was doing much better. The fever had subsided, but he still could not get up or move his arm. Evart gave Ina and Uralda advice for German's care but ended by saying: "If he gets worse, then send Geron for me and I will come."

Evart encouraged everyone to be optimistic. To Geron he said: "I will invite you at the next new moon to come to the Druids' Holy Place for the Festival of Sacrifice. You may take part in place of your father. German should not get on a horse before the next full moon." Geron held the Druid's beautiful white horse so that he could mount. A handshake, words of thanks, a wink, and soon the rider had disappeared into the forest.

Sacrifice at the Druid Holy Place

Geron had much work waiting for him to fill in for his father. While building the new house, the wood-gathering for the winter had been neglected. Geron and German had planned to do that together. At the wood chopping site in the forest there were huge piles of branches waiting to be chopped into firewood. Also, a few sheep still needed shearing. Gerwin looked after the cattle, cut the autumn grass and let it dry in the sun for winter hay. The women looked after the sheep and harvested the last carrots from the field. Gerda gathered mushrooms with Uralda to dry for the winter, also beechnuts and wild berries.

The new moon was approaching. Geron asked his father: "What should I do? There is still so much work to be done, but Evart invited me to go to the sacrifice at the new moon at the Druids' Holy Place." German answered: "You should not miss your first invitation to take part. As a bear hunter you will be initiated into the brotherhood of men for the first time. I have thought about it. How would it be if we asked Wugo to lend us his Roman slave once more? We could exchange some bear meat for the slave. What do you say?"

A feeling of happiness rose up in Geron. He thought: "Finally, Virtus can tell me about the Romans!" To his father he said: "That is a good idea. I will sleep in the old house with the slave and Waldo so that he does not try to run away." So it was settled.

German said: "Geron, sit down by me. I want to tell you about the customs you must uphold at the Holy Place of the Druids. You know the way there because it is close to where Evart and the Druids live. This evening before you go to bed, go down to the stream. You must wash with sand and water from head to toe. The gods must be met with cleanliness and purity. After you have washed go to a deeper part of the stream and kneel down in the water. Say the three high names of WODAN – WILE – WE and dip your face in the water after each name is spoken and keep it there as long as you have breath. Then go to bed and do not speak a word to anyone. Tomorrow morning wash only your hands and face. But don't forget to say the three names just as you did the night before. I would love to ride with you since it's your first time at the ceremony, but, it's not to be. Evart will escort you in. And you will need a sword, so I will lend you mine, and the shield also. Get them down from the wall."

Geron retrieved his father's weapon and shield and brought them over to him. His father told him how to polish the blade with damp ashes and tree bark. Geron went straight to work and put some wolf's fat on the blade after it was polished. Geron asked: "Father, where did you get this sword?"

German answered: "When I was a little older than you are now, I had raised a young colt. I brought it to Hamarson the blacksmith. He traded me the horse for the sword. Not long after that the Romans attacked us at Tütoburg. They wanted to destroy our holy places and turn us into Romans. I was there when we destroyed their legions. This blade brought many a Roman soldier to his death. Since then we Germans have had peace. There have been only small raids from time to time. But, go now, Geron! Make everything ready. Don't forget to wear your bear teeth necklace. Mother and Gerda put a lot of effort into it. You can be proud to wear it."

The next day when Geron was mounted on his horse and ready to go, all the family stood around him to wish him a good journey. Suddenly Uralda let out a scream and pointed toward the house. There stood German in the doorway. He was up for the first time since he had been injured. He held his wounded arm pressed close to his body with his good arm.

German said: "I have to give Geron a blessing for the trip. Give me the sword!" Geron handed it to him. German made the sign of Tyr above the sword. He said: "Give me the shield!" And he made the same sign. "Hurry now! Greet Evart for me and tell him Uralda has taken good care of the wound. It is almost closed."

Geron rode away. Waldo had to be held back by Gerwin or he would have run after Geron. Father said: "You'd better tie him up or he'll run after him a long way."

Geron reached his destination by early afternoon. There were already a number of warriors camping at the edge of the forest. They were grazing their horses on the meadow. Three boys without weapons were standing guard over the horses so they would not go near the Holy Place. Not even a leaf could be eaten from that place.

Geron let his horse drink from the stream, eat some grass, and then he tied it to a nearby post. He walked up to a group of men who were sitting on the ground listening to the old clan leader, Iso. Iso was wearing a golden neck band and a helmet with steer horns on it. Geron loved to listen to what the men were saying. Iso was telling about a feud with the Romans. He paused in his story when he saw Geron take a seat and waved at him to come nearer. Geron went with some embarrassment, his sword at his right hand and the shield on his left.

Iso said: "Boy, you seem to be a little young. Where did you get the sword and shield? What is your name? Where is your father?" Everyone looked with anticipation at the youth who was wearing bear teeth around his neck.

Geron spoke with humility but in a clear voice: "My name is Geron, son of German. My father was badly injured during a bear hunt. He could not accompany me here but he gave me his sword and shield. The Druid Evart invited me to take part in today's sacrifice at the Holy Place."

Iso looked at the boy with kindness, but the questions were not yet over. He said: "What is with those bear teeth? Did you also get them from your father?"

Geron quickly replied: "No, I was there at the bear hunt. The bear clawed my father's shoulder after I had stabbed him with my dagger. I was able to kill the bear with my spear and ax."

Surprised murmuring spread among the men. Iso wanted a closer look at the bear teeth. He said: "That must have been some big bear! How is your father?"

Geron answered: "Evart saved his arm. We are so thankful to him!"

Geron had just spoken when he heard a voice calling: "There he comes now!" There were three white horses just coming into view. In the front was Evart and behind him two other Druids followed by student helpers. The warriors all stood up, took their weapons in hand, and greeted the priests with their sword blades upon their shields. Geron did as the others.

The Druid Elder, an honorable, tall man with a silver-white beard, acknowledged the greeting and said: "Those who are coming to the Holy Place for the first time should now step forward with their escorts." Besides Geron there were five young men there for the first time, but Geron was the youngest. He stood alone. Evart dismounted his horse and stepped forward to be Geron's escort.

The Druid Elder held an intricately carved staff in his hand. He touched the head of every newcomer with it, as well as his right and left shoulder. He murmured words of greeting.

Only then did the other Druids dismount. They stood by the entrance to the Holy Place. The Elder walked in front carrying the sacrificial sword, Evart walked behind the Elder, and the third Druid behind him. Those carrying the coals and other essential implements brought up the rear of the procession. Strong men led the steer to be sacrificed, and behind them, came the warriors. They all walked with heads bowed into the Holy Place which was a wood of oak trees. Nobody said a word. There was a simple wooden fence along the outside perimeter. But not one person would have thought to enter the wooded area without being accompanied by a priest.

The trees had been growing here undisturbed since time immemorial. Geron was in awe at the huge, powerful trunks of the trees. The branches in the crowns of the trees had interwoven to form an impressive canopy that kept the Holy Place in half-darkness. In the middle stood the oldest oak tree and the sacrificial altar. A breeze rustled through the leaves, the breath of Wodan.

The container carrying the hot coals spread a heady perfume in the air that smelled of pine resin and herbs. Geron felt as if he had stepped into another world. He started suddenly. A loud noise resounded. It was the steer. Was he greeting the altar? In their white robes the Druids stepped forward to the altar. The animal was tied to a post. The men effortlessly arranged themselves in a circle.

While the fire was being lit on the altar, Geron looked around and saw the bleached skulls of steers and bears hanging from the lower branches. There were some elk antlers as well.

Suddenly the coals burst into flames. The voice of the Druid bard began to sing in long, drawn-out tones. The men silently lay down their weapons in front of them on the ground. They each made a fist with their left hand and covered it with their right hand. The fire was fed more wood, and the Elder Druid cried out: WODAN – WILE – WE!

All the men repeated this. Then all the deep voices said in unison: "Wodan with us! Wile with us! We with us!" The white-haired Druid spoke into the fire and smoke:

Heal those who sing,
Heal those who can,
Heal those who learn,
Heal those who hear!

The bard took up his song again while the steer, crowned with ivy, was prepared for the sacrifice. The Elder stepped toward the steer. A well-placed thrust of the sword and the steer's life blood flowed into the waiting container. The priest took a branch dipped in the blood, briefly passed it through the fire, and sprinkled it on the initiates who had gathered around the altar. He called each one by his name, and then he sprinkled some of the blood on all the other men who were assembled.

Geron had some drops of blood on his face and hands which he had held in front of his chest. But nobody wiped them away. What blood was on their hands, the men put to their lips. The strongest men now helped to butcher the sacrificed animal. The Elder tossed some of the entrails into the fire.

And then something happened that surprised Geron. After the skin was removed from the animal, it was spread on the ground with the hair side down. Evart removed his white robe and lay down on the skin. Others wrapped it around him leaving only a small opening for him to breathe. All the men knelt down with their foreheads to the ground. Geron did this also along with the other initiates. In the silence only the crackling of the fire and the rustling of the leaves could be heard. This lasted so long that Geron almost felt faint. Finally the Elder gave the signal that they could rise.

Evart stood by the altar in priest's robes. It seemed to Geron that he was deathly pale with wide-opened eyes that looked beyond everything as if he were gazing into other worlds. Evart raised his voice and spoke. Geron had difficulty following all the words, but he heard about the return of the sun god, Baldur.

The meat was cut into pieces and put on a spit to roast. The men sat on their shields. They used their drink horns to get warm blood from the large kettle into which some mead had also been poured. The men drank to friendship. The conversations began. The earnestness of the earlier ceremony gradually gave way to a mirthful gathering with lots of food and drink. The Druids and their students mixed in with the crowd. They listened to the men's stories about what they and their families had done. They gave advice when asked.

Hamarson, the old blacksmith, sat down next to Geron. He wanted to take a look at German's sword that he had made many years before. He said to Geron: "Bring this sword to my smithy sometime. It should be put to the coals and hammered out again."

Geron asked Hamarson: "How do you make chains?"

Hamarson replied: "First you cut rounded iron into equal lengths. Then you fire it, hammer, and bend the lengths into separate rings, one after the other."

Geron asked again: "Can the chains be removed?"

Hamarson said: "Yes, the best thing to do is get them red hot again. But, though it's difficult, it can be done cold with a hammer and an ax. But why are you asking me so many questions about chains? Would you like to become a blacksmith?"

Geron blushed and answered: "I'm very interested in iron things. I think I would like being a blacksmith."

Hamarson said: "Right now I still have an apprentice, but when he is finished with his apprenticeship, I will remember you. I like you, Geron."

The sun went down and the festivities came to an end. Geron thought over whether he should ride back home that night. Evart came up to him and said: "Geron, I invite you to stay this night at the Druid farm. There is enough straw for you in the horse stable."

Geron put two of the large kettles on his horse and took them back to the farm. He made a soft straw bed next to his horse. But he had trouble falling asleep because he was thinking back on the wonderful events of the day. He felt as if the invisible world of the gods had come very close to him that day.

Virtus Is Borrowed Once More

Geron awakened early the next morning. He had to look around for a few seconds before he remembered where he was. It was the first time he had ever been in a strange place by himself overnight. He left the stable with his horse and saw some of the Druids' white horses on the pasture. Geron washed in the fountain and let his horse graze. Before he left he wanted to go up to Evart's cave and thank him. He was secretly hoping to find out more about why Evart had been wrapped up in the steer skin yesterday at the ceremony.

He tied his horse to a tree before he started the climb up to Evart's cave. He had just stepped onto the path when he heard the cawing of Evart's raven who announced every visitor.

So, the Druid was waiting at the cave entrance and greeted Geron merrily: "Wonderful that you stopped by on your way home!" He invited Geron into his cave home. He offered him a cup of milk from the farm and a small bowl of oatmeal. Evart asked: "How did you fare yesterday at the ceremony?"

Geron answered: "I found everything to be wonderful and I will never forget it. It seems to me that I look at the world differently since yesterday. I am so grateful to you, Evart, that you invited me. If I can ever do anything for you, please tell me!"

Evart said: "Perhaps you have a question or two about some of the things you saw yesterday? Or did anything seem strange to you?"

Geron said: "I am puzzled about something. Why did you let yourself be wrapped in the animal skin?"

The Druid was not surprised by this question. He answered: "You know that we Druids are taught to look into the other world from time-to-time, into the world of the gods. When a Druid is wrapped in the skin of an animal that was living a short time before, then the skin is still radiating life. This life is still radiating out into the world and the soul of the Druid can use this energy to go out of his physical body. In this way the soul can go into the other world and observe the creative god forces for a shorter or longer period of time. It is a great and sacred experience." Geron remembered that he had seen Evart very pale with shining eyes, and he felt that he should ask him no more questions about this experience.

Evart abruptly said: "Geron, you have a secret worry. If you need my advice you know where to find me."

Geron was very startled at this. Could Evart read his thoughts? Did he know about Virtus? No, he could not talk about it now because he was not yet sure himself how everything might turn out.

After a pause he said: "I thank you, Evart. The main thing is that Father is getting well. You have given him back his life. I will never forget it." He said his goodbye rather quickly so that he could get home in time to chop more firewood.

Geron started out at a fast pace and was home by midday. He gave German a short report about the events of the day before and gave him Hamarson's greeting and Evart's good wishes. But then he said: "Mother invited Runege for a visit to the new house. I could go over to Wugo's right now and bring her back. Then we could make a deal with her about the Roman slave, and see if he could help me for a week with the firewood as we discussed. Wugo will do whatever Runege says."

German and Ina agreed to his suggestion and so, after a short rest, he rode off again. When he reached Wugo's farm he noticed that the dogs were tied up. Even though they were barking furiously, nobody came out of the house.

As usual, Geron tied his horse to a fence post. He saw that Runege and Wugo were just finishing up shearing a sheep. He greeted them and brought Mother's invitation for a visit to Runege.

She agreed immediately and said: "It comes just at the right time! I have sheared enough sheep for one day! I will come with you right away. Is that all right, old man?"

Wugo nodded his agreement. Geron noticed that he still limped. Runege was making herself ready inside the house and Geron took the opportunity to tell Wugo about the bear hunt and his father's injury. Wugo listened intently to Geron. Nothing interested him more than hunting stories. He did make a sour face when he heard that the Druid had stayed with them for three days. But when he realized that the old house was full of bear meat, he smacked his lips.

Geron casually asked: "Where are Bur and Bor?"

Wugo answered: "Bor is looking after the cattle and Bur is in the woods with the slave. We've got more than enough wood for the winter, but the servants have to have work enough to sweat once in a while." Wugo grinned. He called to Runege in the house: "So, old woman, dress yourself nicely! You have the privilege of riding out with a handsome young man. You can take the mule!"

It was an odd-looking pair that reached German's house in the early afternoon. Geron helped Runege off her mule. Ina gave her a friendly greeting. When Runege saw German lying on the straw with his bandaged shoulder she wanted to put cow manure on it right away. But German said: "For this we have only one helper and that is Evart. He saved not only my arm, but my life as well. Unfortunately, I will not be able to work for a long time and our winter firewood supply is meager. Runege, I would like to ask a favor of you and Wugo."

Runege was afraid he would ask her for firewood, but instead he said: "Our Geron needs a strong man to help him in the forest. Would you loan us the Roman slave again for one week? I would gladly pay you in bear meat."

Runege agreed to the deal, but wanted to take the meat home with her that day. German said: "Let it remain here for another week in the smoke so that it is well cured."

After Runege had examined and admired every corner of the new house, she wanted to go have a look at the bear meat hanging in the old house. Geron took her there. The last of the bear claws was hanging in the smoke. Runege wheedled: "Wugo would run around the house three times on his knees for a bear claw. Give it to me!" Geron got down the prize and gave it to her.

It was getting towards evening when Geron returned with Runege to Wugo's farm. She dangled the bear claw in front of Wugo and said: "There's more bear meat to come, but the slave will have to help Geron with the wood chopping for a week first."

Wugo asked: "Where will you keep him at night? I always lock him up with the swine."

Geron replied: "He can sleep in our old house. I will guard him." Wugo was satisfied. He took Geron into the house to show him a spear that he had once used to kill a bear.

Outside the commotion of the returning wood choppers could be heard. Geron went out to see. He went up behind Virtus, who did not see him, and called out: "Virtus!" Virtus turned around lightning fast, opened his arms wide, and in the next moment would have given Geron a big hug. But he remembered his place suddenly and stopped before it happened. So instead he knelt down and grabbed Geron's knees. Geron ordered him to stand up because Wugo had just come out of the house.

It was good that Wugo had not seen how Virtus greeted Geron. Virtus hung his head in shame as if waiting for Geron to hit him. But nothing of the kind happened. Geron spoke gently: "Virtus, I'm taking you with me for one week to work for us."

Virtus lifted his face, pressed his lips together, swallowed hard, and said: "Geron good!" His dark eyes were shining with gratitude.

Wugo walked up to them. He pushed his fist into Virtus's ribcage and said: "Go, you stinker, and wash yourself in the stream. You stink like a sow. You cannot go to German smelling like that." Virtus went down to the stream with chains rustling. Wugo said to Geron: "I give you my permission to whip him everyday as much as you want because he is better about working when he has felt the whip or the stick. But don't punch an eye out because then he would be worth less in a trade." Wugo grinned and Geron remained silent. But on the inside, Geron had such a rage boiling up in him that he could not quite explain it. He found it disgusting to feel joy at another's pain. But he made sure he did not show any emotion outwardly. He resolved to find some way to free Virtus from Wugo, but he just did not know how to do it.

Wugo asked: "Do you have a whip at home for the horses?"

Geron replied with disdain: "No, my father taught them to obey voice commands. We do not need a whip."

Wugo said: "Then I will loan you one of mine to use on the Roman. When he returns I'll show you how to use it." Wugo disappeared into the house and came back with a leather whip. He gave it to Geron to try: "Runege braided it out of leather. Look, the slave is returning. You can try out the whip on his back."

Virtus came back from his cold bath carrying his clothing on his arm with only a linen cloth bound around his waist so that he could dry off in the air. Wugo let out a whistle. Virtus came running. Wugo told him: "Lie down with your face to the ground." Virtus gave Geron, who was holding the whip, a fearful look and fell to the ground. Wugo cried: "So, Geron show us your strength! Whip him!"

But Geron did not whip him. He wrapped the leather whip around his arm and spoke very calmly: "Wugo, I will not take a slave with me who has been beaten until he can no longer work."

Wugo was visibly disappointed so he kicked Virtus and ordered: "Stand up! You are Geron's slave for one week!" Wugo went and got the ax for Geron that he had promised. Soon the two rode away from Wugo's farm. Geron was riding in front and Virtus sitting sideways behind him. He held the leg irons in his left hand and with his right hand he held onto Geron's shoulder so he would not fall off the horse. They were both silent for a long time. Geron was the first to speak. He asked: "Are you seated all right? Is it good like that?"

Virtus said he was fine. Then he asked: "Geron why did you not hit me with whip like Wugo?"

Geron answered: "Because I did not want to hit you and I will never hit you." Geron glanced back at Virtus and saw that he had tears in his eyes. The ride continued in silence until they reached German's house.

Geron went inside and got the second ax and went with Virtus into the forest. They both began to chop thick branches into smaller pieces for firewood. Virtus worked well with Wugo's ax, so well that Geron could hardly keep up with him. They worked until sundown and there was a large pile of wood to show for it. When they got back to the house, Geron told Virtus to wait outside. Inside he spoke to his father: "The Roman worked hard today. May he eat the evening meal with us, Father?"

German answered: "If you like, it's fine with me. But after we eat he must go back to the old house as we agreed." Geron brought Virtus inside. Uralda put some oatmeal into an extra bowl for the slave. She felt that it was not seemly to eat from the same bowl as a Roman. She put his food a little to one side. The rest of the family ate out of another bowl with their wooden spoons. They were not accustomed to having a stranger in the house who could not be honored as a guest.

Right after the meal Geron said: "I'm going over to tend to the smoke in the old house and will stay there overnight. It was a long day!" He got up and bade Virtus and Waldo go with him. Since it was very dark outside Geron took Virtus by the hand to guide him so he would not trip over his chains. Geron himself knew the way blindfolded.

Geron added some wood to the fire. It should not burn too much so instead there would be a lot of smoke going up to the rafters where the bear meat was hanging. Both boys sat down by the hearth. Geron asked: "Virtus, would you tell me about your life in Rome and who your parents are? How did you come to be captured?"

Virtus began somewhat haltingly: "My father is high soldier and lives with mother and sister in Castra Vetera. Many, many houses, market, temple, Romans say urbs. Big water flows there by name Rhine. My father over many soldiers. Romans say legions. My father gave me horse. I ride with two soldiers to look around Alesia. Seven days we must ride and made night camp on the water Lupia. German soldiers attack us. One Roman killed, two became slaves. Wugo bought me. Bad luck for me. Father, mother surely believe Virtus is dead. Geron, you are a good person. You help that I not get hit!"

Geron asked: "Why do the Romans want German territory?"

Virtus answered: "Roman Emperor believe he is big like god and will govern all lands. The Romans build stone houses. In Roman urbs there are big stone temples for the gods."

Geron asked: "Romans also have German slaves. Are they not also beaten?"

Virtus answered: "German slaves I have seen have no chains. Many are soldiers. Many build houses and work farms. Romans beat only lazy slaves. Many German slaves not want to go back Germany."

Geron heard much more that night around the hearth fire. Then he said: "Let us go to sleep now. Tomorrow we have much work waiting for us."

Virtus lay down in the straw against the wall and thought: "How wonderful to not have to sleep with the pigs tonight!"

Geron added some more wood to the fire for the night. Waldo was ordered to the door to stand guard. Geron also barricaded the opening with some pieces of wood because the bear meat could attrack wild animals.

Geron sat down again next to the glowing fire and thought about the day gone by. In the morning he had been with Evart, the noble Druid, later with the ugly Wugo who tortured Virtus, and now he was in charge of the actions of another human being. Tomorrow evening he wanted to get a closer look at those chains. He had an idea that he might be able to break them, free Virtus from Wugo, and ride with him for seven days to return him to his parents. He listened in the direction where Virtus was and heard his regular breathing. He slept.

Ina had given Geron a sleeping cover made from sheepskins sewn together. The nights had become rather cool. Was it right that he had a warm cover while Virtus would be freezing by morning? He tossed a few sticks into the fire so that it would give light for a short time. He walked over to the straw. He lay down next to the sleeping boy and spread his sheepskin blanket over both of them. Then he was overcome with tiredness as well and fell asleep.

Once Geron awoke in the middle of the night and felt Virtus's hand on his chest. He thought: "How strange. If Virtus was a German I would become blood brothers with him. But Roman and German blood do not mix. Would the day ever come when it did?" He turned on his side and snuggled into the blanket.

Waldo was sleeping peacefully. Geron pulled back the cover a little. Outside he could see the shining stars. Two of them were very close together. Evart had called them "The Twins." Underneath he could see the bright Sirius. Geron thought: "Even the stars have friendships!

A flight in the night would be possible when Sirius was shining." He put some more wood on the fire.

When he got back under the covers Virtus gave a sudden cry from a bad dream: "No, No!"

Geron thought that he must be dreaming about Wugo's whippings. He said: "Virtus, it's me, Geron!"

Virtus woke up and whispered slowly: "Geron, you with me!" But he fell asleep again immediately.

Geron was now very certain: "I will help Virtus get free!"

Geron could see the morning light shining through the smoke hole in the roof. He got up, walked to the entrance and took away the barrier. Waldo gave him a joyful greeting.

Virtus crawled out from under the warm sheepskins, stretched his limbs, and said: "Geron, that was best night in Germany! Today Virtus work very hard for you!" Geron told him to put some more wood on the fire and went to get some breakfast for both of them at the new house. Uralda had already milked the goats.

Gerwin remarked to Geron: "I want to go with you and Virtus into the woods today. It's boring here. Gerda, Mother, and Uralda can get along without me." Geron thought about the fact that there was only one week to get all of the wood in for the winter. So he decided to take Gerwin with him.

Geron asked Uralda to give him some old woven rags. She asked: "For what do you want them?"

He replied: "You never know if you will need a bandage for a wound when you're working with an ax." However, once they were in the forest, Geron gave the rags to Virtus and told him to wrap the leg irons in the fabric so they would not chafe his skin.

When Gerwin saw how the two older boys were skillfully working at a good tempo, he also got into the rhythm with his little ax and kept up with them quite well. At midday Geron said to him: "Gerwin, go and get some food! Bring Father's horse back with you and you can begin to carry some wood back to the house this afternoon."

That evening there was a good amount of wood stacked under the overhanging eaves on the side of the house. German, who was slowly getting back on his feet, was very happy to see that the wood pile needed for the winter was growing even without his help.

The following morning Geron and Virtus were again sitting around the fire. Virtus had become more trusting. The anxiety in his eyes was almost completely gone. But the thought that the beautiful days with Geron would soon be coming to an end put a damper on his mood.

Geron suddenly said: "Let me see how the blacksmith made your leg irons!" Virtus put one of his feet on Geron's knee and Geron examined the chain link by link. The largest iron ring was next to the foot cuff and the smaller rings in the chain were attached to it. Geron took a knife and tried to see if he could get the blade in where the iron rings were pressed together. It worked with most of them. Virtus looked with wonder at how carefully Geron examined everything.

Geron asked: "Virtus, have you never thought of escape?" Virtus was silent and looked at Geron with uncertainty. Geron said: "Speak. You may tell me everything."

Virtus began to talk. "Every Roman slave in Germany thinks of escape. But with chains one cannot walk. Dogs are chasing. Even without chains the way too long. There are forests, German hunters, bears, slave not find the way. On river are fishers. Roman slave known by dark hair, whipped, and killed." Virtus became very sad and was silent once again.

Geron resolved anew to help Virtus escape. He said: "At the end of the week, when the winter wood supply is finished, I will help you get away from Wugo and never have to return."

Geron was shocked at the effect his words had on Virtus. Virtus became pale. His hands shook. Finally, he said: "Geron you make fun. I'm sad."

Geron realized that Virtus thought he was having fun with him about Wugo. He took Virtus's hand, looked him in the eye, and assured him: "Virtus, I am serious. I want to help you! That is why I examined your chains so closely. I think I can break them with the ax."

Now Virtus understood that Geron was not kidding. His face regained its color. He said a little breathlessly: "When I flee, German men catch me and kill me!"

Geron had already thought about this. He answered: "Virtus, I will not let you go alone through the forests. My horse is strong. I will ride with you and bring you to your parents in Castra Vetera."

Virtus stared into the fire. Geron saw that he was struggling for words. Finally, he said: "Geron, this is beautiful dream. When dream come true, Father give you gold and silver and can pay Wugo. My father is rich. What will your father say?"

That was worrying Geron, too. He said: "We must finish all the firewood this week. The last evening we will break the chains. On the seventh morning we will go early into the forest and in the evening, instead of riding back to Wugo's farm, we will ride away from here. I will take some bear meat with us for rations. If we meet anyone, we will change directions. You must tell me the name of a different Roman town. If Wugo tries to follow us they will go in the wrong direction. Is there another Roman town not too far from Castra Vetera?"

Virtus said: "There is the town of Colonia."

Geron said: "Good, I will remember that name. But how do we find Castra Vetera?"

Virtus explained: "First comes River Lupia. I ride to Lupia when I captured."

Geron said: "That must be what we call the Lipp River. I know the way to its source. We can be there in one night on the horse. But let us get some sleep now. Tomorrow morning we will begin early with the wood."

It was hard to believe how much the boys worked the next few days, from dawn to dark. From then on Geron always took his horse into the forest with Virtus riding behind him so the horse would become used to the double load. On the fifth evening Geron said to Virtus: "Today I will try to break your leg chains. I don't feel good about leaving it until the last evening."

Virtus protested: "Gerwin will see me without chains!"

Geron retorted: "Gerwin will see nothing. I will tie the broken chains with bear intestines. Since the bear hunt Father and I have been good friends. He will understand and not be angry with me for long. He knows Wugo!"

Geron had brought a thick piece of an oak branch with him from the forest. It was the hardest wood. He lay it next to the fire. He told Virtus to put his foot on the oak so that the large ring lay on top of the cuff on his foot. He used the Roman ax as a chisel and his own ax as a hammer. After a few well-aimed blows the chain began to come apart. Geron was careful not to miss the mark and injure Virtus's leg. When the chisel ax reached the wood underneath, finally, he was able to free one foot!

Both boys had sweat on their brows, one because of the difficult work, and the other because of the anxiety. Virtus could now move his left foot freely for the first time in a year. He grabbed Geron by the shoulders and said: "Geron, well done! Now the other foot!" The second ring was a little easier.

Geron was just getting ready to deliver the last blows when he heard Waldo barking outside. German's voice could be heard: "What are you chopping in there? Quiet down, we can't get to sleep for the noise!"

Geron said quickly: "We're almost finished, Father. We're going to sleep now. Good night!" All was still. German had gone back inside. For the next few blows with the ax Geron put some leather on the blade to muffle the noise.

When both legs were free Virtus jumped up and down a few times. He felt as light as air. He laughed through his tears, hugged Geron, threw himself in the straw, hammered his fists on the floor, and gave Geron cause to worry about his sanity. Finally he quieted down and crawled under the blanket. Geron could hear him sobbing.

Geron climbed up to the rafters and cut off two pieces of the smoked bear meat. He took some of the intestine string and tied it to the iron cuff so that everything would be ready for tomorrow. Then he lay down next to Virtus. What was wrong with him? He did not say anything. Geron could hear him breathing heavily. He asked: "Virtus, what's wrong?"

But instead of answering Virtus suddenly put his arms around Geron. He said: "Geron, I am very happy and very afraid. What will you say when German warriors meet us?"

Geron replied: "I will say you are my slave. I am a German with a bear teeth necklace, initiated at the Altar of Tyr! They will leave us alone. And I have the weapons with me! If we later meet up with Romans, then you must do the talking." Virtus was satisfied with this explanation. He had complete faith in Geron.

The next morning Geron tied the chains back onto the cuffs. Gerwin was kept busy hauling wood and he did not notice any changes in the leg irons. Virtus was supposed to be returned to Wugo the next day.

The Escape

Their last evening in the old house had arrived. Geron kindled a bright fire to give light during the preparations. In an ancient trunk that had been left in the house after the move Geron hid the slave chains. He took a pair of old pants that had belonged to his father from the trunk and gave them to Virtus to wear. They were long and would cover the scars made by the leg irons. There was also an old fur cap for Virtus. For weapons Geron took a spear and an old shield as well as the short knife his father had given him after the bear hunt. He put on his necklace of bear teeth. He also put on the cap that his mother had sewn for him from bear fur for the coming winter. Everything was now ready for their secret journey

Suddenly Waldo barked. Geron had tied him to a post outside and also the horse not far from him. Someone was coming. The skin over the door was raised. Gerda walked in. In her hand she was carrying a loaf of freshly baked bread. She had an amazed look on her face when she saw her brother looking like a warrior and Virtus in long pants. She knew the slave could not put on long pants while he was wearing the chains. Virtus quickly dived into the straw. No chains could be heard. Geron was so surprised by his sister's sudden entrance that he could not speak. His sister asked: "Where are you going?"

Geron replied: "We're going for a night ride!"

Gerda asked further: "Dressed as a warrior? And Virtus without chains?" Gerda had often felt sympathy for the slave with the dark, sad eyes. That is why she noticed the lack of chains right away.

Geron knew his sister well. He walked up to her, took both her hands in his, and said: "Gerda, I am going to tell you a secret. But you must swear by Tyr that you will not say anything about this until tomorrow evening."

She answered: "Geron, I will do it for you. I swear by Tyr to be silent about it until tomorrow evening!"

Geron went on: "Go to Mother and tell her thanks for the bread. Nothing else. Do not say anything about what you have seen here or what I am about to tell you. I am taking Virtus back to his father in the Roman town of Colonia. I took off the chains. His father will pay me ransom money. I will pay Wugo later with Roman silver. When I will come back is uncertain. I will speak with Father when I return. But you must be quiet. They will think that I took Virtus back to Wugo. You may only speak when Wugo shows up to claim Virtus. Be brave and quiet." He pressed Gerda close and stroked her hair.

She got tears in her eyes at the thought of losing her brother forever. She whispered: "Geron, I will pray to Freya to help you! Come back soon!"

Geron put the fresh bread into his leather pouch with the bear meat. Virtus had gotten up off the floor. Geron waved him over. "Let us get on the horse!"

Virtus grabbed Gerda's hand and pressed it to his forehead as was the Roman custom and said: "Gerda, dear girl, I thank you for your silence!" Gerda took Waldo with her into the old house so that he would not bark. There was no sound to be heard as the two rode away.

The night ride led in the direction of the source of the Lipp River. In the sky above Sirius, the Twins, and a half-full moon shone brightly. Gerda made her way slowly back to the new house. She was glad that nobody came to check on her at the old house. She brought Mother the thank-you from Geron for the bread and went to her sleeping place right away. But she could not sleep. Gerda's thoughts were on the two riders in the night. She silently whispered her prayer: "Freya, be with them, Freya. Lead Geron and Virtus, Freya. Protect them from accidents and wild animals!"

Geron was familiar with the path from his home to the source spring of the Lipp River. Their most precious possession right now was the horse. Geron let it have free rein without forcing him. Brenno, the horse, had a heavy enough load with the two boys. Sometimes he broke into a trot. From time to time the boys would guide Brenno to a clearing and let him catch his breath and chew a little dew-damp grass. The friends spoke hardly a word to one another and so they were both filled with their own thoughts.

At such a rest stop, Virtus suddenly whispered: "I see a dark form over there!" It is moving." Geron looked and saw it also. He stood, took hold of his spear and called: "Hali!" There was no answer. Was it a person, a bear, or something else? The horse was showing no concern.

Geron spoke quietly to Virtus: "Hold the horse!" He tried to sharply focus he eyes and walked toward the form. He hid behind a big rock and threw a stone in the direction of the dark form. It sounded like wood. Geron gave a sigh of relief. It was nothing but an old tree trunk. And the branch of a tree behind it was waving in the wind.

This little experience had the effect of lightening their mood so that they could relax a little after the tension of the last several hours. They reached the spring in the gray dawn. They cupped their hands and drank the fresh, cold water in large gulps. They ate some of the bread and smoked meat. Brenno drank his fill and began grazing contentedly . Virtus asked worriedly: "Will Gerda really not say anything?"

Geron replied: "Gerda keeps her promises. Before this evening nobody will now about our escape, and by that time we will be far away!" Geron had just said this when they heard voices and horses hooves coming their way.

Virtus jumped up: "Run!"

Geron ordered: "No, sit down! Act like it's nothing. Pull the cap over your hair and cover your beard with your hands!" Three German warriors came riding up to the spring to rest and let their horses drink. In the dim light they had not noticed that someone was already there. Geron said a cheerful "Hali" which was returned with a surprised "Halo."

The strangers withdrew a little to drink some water from the spring. One of them stood up and walked toward Geron and Virtus. Geron whispered urgently: "Remain sitting and don't talk!"

Geron stood up and greeted the man with a handshake. The German asked: "Only one horse for two people? Are you hunting?"

Geron answered: "Yes, sir, we are on a hunt."

The two other men also joined the group out of curiosity. They had seen Geron's bear teeth necklace. One of them said: "Did you kill it yourself?"

Geron replied: "Yes, with my father."

Another man said: "Your companion has no weapon?"

Geron said: "He is my servant. He can carry the meat back home on his shoulders." They all three laughed.

One said: "Good luck! Don't go too far down river or you'll come too close to the Roman castle. The Romans like to capture young Germans." They returned to their horses and rode away.

Virtus said: "Well done, Geron!"

They drank some more water and Virtus said: "Lupia water flows by Castra Vetera and house of my father!" He splashed his hands in the water happily and washed his face.

Soon they were back on the horse. The day was slowly becoming brighter. While they were riding along Geron once again heard the sound of approaching horses. This time he guided Brenno into the forest and off the path until the riders were past them. They were both tired from the long night ride. They decided to rest a little further in the woods out of sight of the path. They both felt much better after a short nap. They started off again on untrodden paths, always keeping the river in sight as they descended into the valley.

Towards evening they started looking for a good camping site somewhere out of sight in the bushes but close to the water. They were fortunate that the weather was dry so they could lie on the moss and leaves because the October nights were cool. Before they went to sleep Geron said: "By this time they will have found out about our escape at home. Gerda can tell them now. Perhaps Wugo is already riding in the direction of Colonia."

Virtus had become very quiet. He said: "The Romans build castles on Lupia River. Soon Virtus can speak Roman language." They had a satisfying meal of bread, meat, and river water. Geron realized that the food would last no longer than one more day.

The Escape Is Discovered

The morning after Geron and Virtus had ridden away, German went to the old house. He wanted to remind Geron that he must return the Roman slave on time to Wugo and to not forget the bear meat. He found no one at the house. The fire was burning very low. Wugo's ax was lying nearby. German thought: "They started out early and he forgot the ax." He looked up to the rafters and could not tell if any meat had been taken, and so he wondered if Geron had forgotten that as well. German shook his head in bewilderment.

When German returned to the new house he reported his unwelcome discovery. Gerda was tending the sheep on the meadow. Gerwin said: "Geron told me he was going to take the slave back very early this morning." Naturally, Gerwin did not know that he was taking the slave back to his home. So nobody thought much more about it since Geron would soon be returning from Wugo's farm. The day wore on. Geron did not return.

It was getting dark. German noticed a rider nearing the house. It was Wugo. He remained seated on his horse, which was against his usual custom, and screamed: "Where is my slave? Where is Geron? He was supposed to bring him back early this morning!"

German was speechless. Gerwin, Ina, and Uralda came running out when they heard the shouting.

Finally German said something: "Geron rode off early this morning. We thought he was returning the slave. He is not here."

Now Wugo became really angry: "The damned wolf! There I was, good enough to loan out my slave with an ax, no less, and the son of German goes for a joy ride with him to have a good time!" Wugo rolled his eyes and shook his fists.

German said: "Wugo, I must ask your forgiveness. I do not understand Geron's actions. I really did think he was taking the slave back to you early this morning." He turned to Gerwin: "Go and get a large piece of bear meat for Wugo!" Gerwin disappeared.

German addressed Wugo: "It could be that they had an accident, or that they rode by the Holding farm. Geron will surely return shortly with the Roman. I'm sorry, Wugo. Please, get off your horse. Ina will make something for you to drink."

Wugo grumbled and mumbled to show his displeasure but he did finally get off his horse. He limped over to Ina and drank from the cup she handed him. As soon as Gerwin returned with the meat, Wugo got right back on his horse. Gerwin handed it up to Wugo. Wugo weighed it in his hands, smelled it, and then said, a little milder: "Tomorrow Geron can come and help me with hunt to pay for the lost day's work. I can shoot all right from horseback but my darned leg doesn't want to cooperate. Geron can chase something for me."

German nodded his agreement: "Yes, I will tell Geron to go to you."

Wugo did not say "Thank-you," and he left without another word.

German went with Gerwin back to the old house. In all of the excitement he had forgotten to give the ax back to Wugo. German glanced up at the wall over the old trunk. Geron's lance and the old shield were missing. Had he put them inside the trunk? He opened the lid and found the slave's leg irons. Now German was certain that the slave had talked Geron into helping him escape! Gerwin saw the chains in his father's hands and exclaimed: "Those are the chains from Virtus!" German told him to take the ax and the chains back to the house. Just then Gerda returned the sheep to the stable.

A little while later German, Ina, Uralda, and Gerwin were all sitting around the hearth fire in the new house. The chains went from hand to hand. When Gerda walked in, Gerwin said to her: "Geron got the chains off Virtus and helped him escape!" Gerda was relieved that she did not have to say anything about what she knew. She was happy to remain quiet.

Uralda lamented: "When he gets to the Romans they will capture him and make either a slave of him or a Roman soldier!"

To everyone's surprise Gerda said: "I don't believe it. Perhaps the Roman parents will be grateful to Geron and pay him ransom money for the return of their son. Geron is brave and clever. He will come back!"

But who should bring the news to Wugo? German said: "I can sit on a horse again. I must ride over to Wugo's house myself and tell him what happened. But tomorrow morning will be soon enough. It would be senseless to ride there and back in the night since we don't even know what direction Geron and Virtus took. Wugo should be able to enjoy his bear meat tonight. The bad news will come soon enough. I can't understand Geron. Now I must bear the brunt of Wugo's anger for his deed. Wugo paid three cows for the slave, and we have only five!"

Ina said: "If only he comes back healthy!"

Uralda ended the conversation by saying: "May the Gods protect Geron. I will make a sacrifice for him."

Before they went to bed, Gerwin spoke to Gerda: "Geron did right. Virtus had a terrible life with Wugo!"

Gerda agreed: "Yes, Geron did right, but I feel sorry for Father that he has to take the news to awful Wugo."

The Roman Castle

Early the next morning Geron and Virtus awoke in their hidden camp. They were very hungry and ate some of the bread and meat right away. Some meat was left over. Geron said: "Today, instead of bread, we must eat mushrooms and beechnuts." They got back to the path that wound along beside the river. There was a ford there. The Romans must have built it. Their legions had come through there to try and force the Germans into battle. German had told his son how he had been there during this battle when he was a youth and how Arminius with the Germans had defeated the Romans in the forests. They had been enemies ever since.

The water of the Lupia was not very deep at this place. The horse had no trouble crossing the ford. Virtus remarked: "Lupia. On other side maybe find Romans and we find castle also." But they rode the whole day without meeting anyone.

Geron thought: "The Germans do not travel too far downriver and no Romans are in sight. This must be border territory." All of the meat had been eaten at midday but with the mushrooms known to Geron and the beechnuts they were able to eat their fill.

It was getting late. Suddenly they heard horses. Geron hesitated. He was not sure if he should ride Brenno out of sight into the forest or ride towards the horses. Too late! The Roman soldiers surrounded them. One of them grabbed Brenno's reins and another sprang from his horse and went for Geron's weapons.

The troop leader said: "Two young Germans! We'll take them with us! Tie them up!" One soldier tried to tear Geron's lance out of his hands but he would not let go.

Then Virtus said loudly in Latin: "Stop, my Roman comrades!" He took off the fur cap. His coal black hair could be clearly seen. Virtus went on: "We have escaped. We need your help. I was captured by the Germans and made a slave. My father is a Roman officer in Castra Vetera."

The soldier was surprised but still skeptical: "And this one? That's a real German, a bear killer!"

Virtus replied: "He is a friend and has risked his life to help me escape back to my homeland."

The soldier asked: "Who is your father in Castra Vetera?"

Virtus declared: "Julus Severus!"

This name worked like magic. The other soldiers dropped the reins of Geron's horse and let go of his lance. They all spoke at once: "Julus Severus! It is the son of Julus Severus! Their leader spoke: "I know Julus Severus. He is our commander. Then you must be his son who disappeared about one year ago."

Virtus answered: "Yes, I am Virtus, the son of Julus Severus, and this is my friend who got me free." In order to dispel any doubts, Virtus raised one pant leg. Then everyone could see the ugly scars from the leg irons.

The Roman leader said: "Soldiers, we will ride back immediately to the castle in Arbalo. Our scouting trip has yielded precious findings." He turned to Virtus and said: "What should we do with your companion, the German? Will he go back now?"

Virtus quickly replied: "No! He will accompany me to Castra Vetera and return me to my father. We have an agreement."

That evening the scouting expedition and the two fugitives rode through the gates of the stone castle Arbalo. Once they reached the inner courtyard soldiers and servants came up from all sides. News had spread rapidly that the son of Julus Severus had been found.

The commander of the outpost, Gaius, was among the group of onlookers. He began speaking with Virtus: "You say you are Virtus, the son of Julus Severus? Tell me what happened!"

Virtus explained how it happened that he and four other Romans had fallen into the hands of the Germans. He could name the leader of his group who had lost his life when they were attacked. He revealed the exact location of his father's house in Castra Vetera.

Gaius had no more doubt that he was standing before the son of the famous commander, Julus Severus. He ordered: "Take Virtus to the provision rooms and give him the robe of a Roman soldier. Then bring him to my living quarters. Let the German youth and his horse go! He should return home."

Virtus contradicted: "Commander Gaius, I have made an agreement with my friend Geron. He will ride with me to my father in Castra Vetera. He is not only my friend, he is my liberator! He should be rewarded."

Gaius nodded: "As you wish, Virtus. But make sure he does not spy on us." With that Gaius returned to his quarters.

Virtus turned to Geron and said: "Geron, you will have my protection. You need not be afraid of the Romans. I will get a horse. Tomorrow we ride to my father. He will be good to you."

Geron nodded. He had remained quiet as a mouse during all this time. The possessions of the Romans – their huge, stone houses, the castle with its mighty walls and outbuildings and the heavy oak door – all of these things made a powerful impression on Geron. He could not get enough of looking at the beautiful horses, the leather equipment, and the shining weapons of the soldiers. He admired the helmets, the breastplates, and the boots. But he could not understand one word that they said. For the first time in his life he experienced what it meant to be a stranger in a strange land.

The quartermaster, the soldier in charge of the weapons, clothes, and other equipment, waved at Virtus to come with him. Virtus took Geron's arm and said: "Geron, come with me." They climbed an artfully constructed stone staircase. Geron had never seen such a thing. They both followed the quartermaster into one of the towers of the castle. It was a huge room filled with weapons of all kinds. Soldiers' clothes were hanging on the walls. Virtus was given a set of clothes. How he enjoyed getting rid of the old clothes! He asked Geron: "Would you like Roman clothes also?"

Geron shook his head: "No, Virtus, I am a German."

Virtus looked at Geron's naked feet, spoke to the quartermaster, and came back with a pair of leather boots for Geron. Geron was happy to accept. He slipped into the boots and walked a few steps on the stone floor. The heals resounded loudly. Geron thought that was funny. He laughed for the first time in many days. At home he was only allowed to wrap his feet in pieces of leather during the coldest winter days.

Virtus had changed his clothes and looked like a real Roman again. The image Geron had of Virtus as the poor slave deserving of his sympathy suddenly disappeared. Could Virtus see that in his eyes? A certain reserve?

Virtus walked up to Geron and hugged him. He said: "Geron, we will always be friends. As Romans and Germans we will be brothers!" The quartermaster was taken aback by this display. He shook his head and could not understand it. But Virtus continued: "Come on, I will show you around the castle."

They returned to the large courtyard and Virtus was ordered to appear before Commander Gaius. He left Geron with the soldiers and did as he was ordered.

Some soldiers were practicing archery next to a long wall. Their target was a straw mat with a black center mark. Geron sidled over to watch the target practice. How often he had practiced with his bow and arrow from the time he was a very young boy. He could even shoot a bird out of the air.

The soldiers were not very good. Some of them did not even hit the straw mat. Suddenly an archer with a bow and three arrows walked up to Geron and said: "German, shoot!"

Geron accepted the challenge. He carefully examined the bow and arrow. It was of much finer construction than the ones made at home. With his first arrow he hit the mat; the second landed close to the black middle; the third hit dead center. The other archers admired Geron's good aim. They brought him more arrows.

After a little while Virtus returned to find Geron with the archers on their way to becoming friends. Virtus said: "Geron, we will ride to Father tomorrow. Gaius gave me a horse. Come on, I'll show you the castle now." He went to a well that stood in the middle of the courtyard. There was a wheel over it which could be used to let down a bucket and bring it up full of water.

Virtus took Geron to one of the cellar rooms which contained the soldier's kitchen. Meat was boiling in huge copper kettles. The smoke was funneled up the chimney and disappeared. Soldiers sat on benches at enormous oak tables eating their evening meal. But all of the Latin being spoken around him went past Geron's ears like so much noise.

At a signal from the commander, the soldiers left the table. Virtus climbed with Geron to the guard post at the top of one of the towers. Two guards were there. The evening was growing darker. Virtus showed Geron the direction from which they had ridden: "Behind that wooded hill lies the Lupia spring and your house."

Geron could see the stars of the Big Dipper in the sky above the place where his home was. Only the stars had come with him. A wave of homesickness overcame him, a longing for his life back in the forest. From this day he knew with certainty that Roman life would always be foreign to him.

Virtus pointed in the opposite direction: "Castra Vetera and my father's house is back there."

Geron thought for a moment: "Should I really ride with Virtus to his home? Or should I go back to my home as fast as possible?" But then he told himself: "I cannot return to Wugo with empty hands. Virtus promised that I would be rewarded and I must bring the money to Wugo." He was also very curious to see a real Roman city.

Virtus said: "Gaius says you should sleep with the soldiers and I with the commanders." Geron wanted to see to his horse before he went to bed. Virtus walked with him. Brenno stood a little to one side in the enormous stable and ate some hay that the stable boy had given to all the horses. When Brenno realized Geron was there he seemed very happy to see him. Virtus got a bucket with some extra oats in it to give to Brenno as a reward for his good service.

Then Virtus led Geron down into the huge dormitory for the soldiers. Thick straw had been strewn on the stone floor. Groups of soldiers were playing dice games in the weak light of several oil lamps. They passed around a drinking mug . Virtus pulled Geron a little away into a corner. Here would be a good place for him to rest his tired limbs. Geron was soon deeply asleep.

He awoke once in the middle of the night. There were two small oil lamps shining weakly. Geron noticed that someone was coming near him. It was Virtus. He whispered: "Virtus can not sleep. He not want to leave Geron alone." Geron realized that a friendly heart can also beat in a Roman breast.

A strange noise awakened Geron early the next morning. He watched in amazement as the Roman soldiers stood up and formed a neat row. At first, Geron also wanted to stand but Virtus held him back and said: "Geron stay here!" Orders were given. The men all stuck their feet into their boots at the same time. The boots had been put into a neat row the night before. Another command and the whole troop marched out the door. Geron's mouth was wide open in bewilderment.

Virtus said: "Geron, we can get up now and feed the horses and ride away." When they arrived in the courtyard there were no soldiers to be seen. Virtus explained: "Soldiers walk to river to wash." Geron noticed that everything here functioned by commands. It was much different in Germany. As much as he was impressed by the castle he thought he could never live behind such thick walls!

Castra Vetera

Commander Gaius accompanied Virtus to the horse stable, pointed at three horses, and said: "Virtus, you can choose one of these three horses. They are well-trained riding horses from important people. They belong to the Roman Army of the Emperor. I will lend one of them to you. Your father will put everything in order." Geron helped Virtus to choose. They decided on a black horse. Two stable boys led out the horse and saddled it with a Roman saddle. Gaius handed Virtus a small leather bag of Roman coins as traveling money.

As they were riding down the hill from the castle they saw the half-naked soldiers returning from their morning bath. Their commander greeted Virtus with a raised hand and Virtus returned the greeting. He said: "If we ride very fast we will be able to gain a day!" The horses broke into a gallop and Geron was happy to see that Brenno was able to keep up with the black Roman horse. Virtus was in a very good mood. He was riding on a Roman road on a Roman horse!

They rode for quite a few hours with very little rest. They came upon a stone building that was very close to the road. Virtus said: "Here tavern. We can eat." There were a few horses tied up in front of the tavern as well as a wagon drawn by two horses. Virtus explained: "They bring flour to castle so soldiers have bread." They tied their horses to the iron rings that were built into the stone wall and walked into the tavern.

Geron was surprised at all the tables and benches inside. Trades-men and soldiers were eating from clay bowls and drinking from mugs. The lively conversation lagged for a moment when Geron and Virtus walked in. What was a blond German doing here? What business had he to be in a Roman tavern? A surly Roman shouted something to Virtus and gave Geron a dirty look. Virtus gave him a cheeky re-sponse. Everyone laughed. The Roman's face got red but he did not say anything. A soldier came laughing up to Virtus and handed him a cup to drink. Virtus passed it on to Geron. It was wine! Geron found it to be sour. He would have preferred milk or water.

He asked Virtus: "What did you say to that man?"

Virtus laughed and said: "He said there was no food for a Ger-man in a Roman tavern and I said it was because he ate enough for seven Germans." Geron had his first meal in a Roman tavern with Roman spoons. But he did not want any "sour water" to drink. The Romans called it vinum. So he got a cup of water instead.

While they were eating Virtus showed Geron the coins he had. He said: "This silver has the head of Emperor Tiberius." Then he showed him another coin: "Here is the Roman wolf. For food we will pay a wolf." Geron did not really understand why that was. In Germany a guest was always fed for nothing in return and here one had to give a picture of a wolf or an emperor's head.

After their meal they rode further. But the horses were spared the galloping when it got towards evening. As it was getting dark they arrived at another tavern. Here they could sleep on the straw.

On the last day of their journey the road was busy with wagons, riders, soldiers, and pilgrims. Geron could see that the landscape was dotted with stone houses and grazing cattle. The road went along beside the river. Suddenly Geron noticed a military rowboat that was traveling very fast on the water. He had never seen such a thing. He stopped his horse and followed the boat with his eyes. Virtus said: "My father also has ship. Geron and Virtus go on water." After a very long ride they came to a large, long bridge under which flowed a wide river. Virtus shouted for joy: "The Rhine!" He pointed to the other side of the river: "Castra Vetera over there. We will be there soon!"

The bridge was guarded by soldiers. They controlled the traffic over the bridge. Two towers and a building were next to the entrance. Virtus walked up to a guard and said: "I have orders from Commander Gaius at Castle Arbalo to go to General Julus Severus." He showed the guard a small wax tablet with some writing on it.

The guard asked: "What about the young German?"

Virtus answered with confidence: "My companion." They were allowed to pass and so they rode over the Rhine River. A cold, autumn wind was blowing across the bridge. Geron thought it was miraculous that one could ride over water. He saw small and large boats on the river and men inside them who were moving the boats forward with wooden shovels.

Virtus suddenly shouted: "Look, Geron, the gates to the city!" A short ride from the bridge and they could see the walled city. Two imposing towers stood one on either side of the gate. In the middle of the entrance was a wide gate for horses and wagons and there were two smaller gates one on either side for those on foot. There was a general buzz of people, wagons, and soldiers. Geron was very confused. But Virtus said: "Ride next to me, Geron. Here is the street to my father's house. Joy! Joy!"

Geron felt as if he was in a dream. He had often ridden through forests and had to pick his way through trees and bushes to find a path. But here, he had to find his way through people, wagons, and other hindrances. He had trouble following Virtus rushing through the crowd.

They came to a wide plaza and Geron saw hundreds of people. Some were sitting on stone steps and others were climbing the steps. At the top of the steps was a large stone building. Its roof was supported by stone columns like tree trunks. Virtus stopped and said: "The house of the Roman god, Jupiter!" Geron thought it strange that Roman gods would live in stone houses when in Germany the gods lived in the clouds, the sun, in lightning, and storm. But he had no time to think about that now because Virtus had gone on ahead.

Suddenly he turned onto a side street up to a large gate. The watchman, an old man, started up and shouted: "Virtus! Virtus! Is it really you?" Virtus jumped from his horse. The old man hugged him and broke into tears. He had known Virtus since he was a baby. The other servants came running when they heard the old man shouting. Geron also got off his horse and was content to be a silent witness to the homecoming. The old, loyal watchmen stumbled into the house to get Virtus' mother. His father was not at home. The servants encircled Virtus. Some of them kissed his hand and some kissed his boots.

A well-dressed noblewoman appeared between two stone columns with two maids at her side. When she saw Virtus she screamed, ran towards him with outstretched arms, and fell sobbing onto his chest. The servants had withdrawn a little distance. Everyone was mystified about the miraculous return of the boy they had thought to be dead. Finally, Julia, his mother, took Virtus by the arm to go back into the house. Virtus hesitated a moment. He pointed to the entrance where Geron was still standing with his horse. He said: "Mother, look, there is my liberator, the one who brought me here."

The Roman woman looked at the blond-haired Geron. He looked a little helpless and forlorn at the moment. Mother said: "Your liberator? What a wonderful boy! Bring him to me!" Virtus instructed a servant to take care of the horses. He went and got Geron and introduced him to his mother. She stood in the middle between the two boys, took both their arms, and walked with them up the steps into the large house.

Geron noticed with curiosity that the woman smelled of flowers. She must be a noblewoman indeed! They walked past a fountain whose water was spraying upward. Geron could not understand how that was possible. The water splashed into a beautiful, large, marble basin. There were white, naked statues made out of stone standing around the fountain. They walked through a large door and Geron was met with a wonderful sense of warmth, but he saw no fire.

The servants and slaves followed at a little distance and held a lively discussion about the unexpected return of the lost son. The kitchen chef hurried to the kitchen with two slaves to prepare food and drink for the hungry travelers.

Mother Julia let go of the boys' arms when they reached the entrance to the inner rooms of the house. The room they entered had a high ceiling and was dimly lit. There was daylight peeking through a few holes. This room was also wonderfully warm, but again Geron could see no fire. Julia and Virtus sat on a divan and indicated that Geron should do the same. Until that day Geron had not sat on anything but rocks or hard, wooden stools. He plumped down on the divan and promptly fell over backwards. The shock caused him to jump up again very quickly. The second time he lowered himself rather gingerly onto the soft cushions. Virtus laughed: "Roman divans are soft, but not dangerous!"

Julia and Virtus began excitedly talking with each other so Geron was free to survey his surroundings unobserved. Suddenly he noticed there were colorful animals on the floor but they did not move. There were human forms on the walls and they did not move either.

Two servants brought food and drink on a beautiful serving tray. Virtus turned to Geron and said: "Father went riding with my sister, Claudia. They will be home this evening. I will show you the house after we eat. Mother is very grateful to you." Geron had dropped a piece of bread on the floor so he bent down to pick it up. He noticed it had fallen on one of the animals but when he felt for it he realized the animal was made of stone and it was warm to the touch. Were there warming stones here? Geron could not explain why the floor was so warm.

Julia was giving instructions to a servant. Virtus said to Geron: "After the meal we will both have baths and get clean clothes, even you!"

Yes, Geron had noticed that his soiled animal skin clothes did not exactly fit in with the finery of this house. Perhaps he smelled badly as well. He asked: "Is it far to the river for bathing?"

Virtus laughed out loud and answered: "Geron, the river is here in the house. A warm river!" Geron wondered if he was talking about the little fountain with the water spraying upward. Did one get into the basin to bathe?

After they finished eating Virtus took Geron with him. Julia gave them both a friendly wave. Geron asked: "Virtus, why is the stone floor so warm?"

His friend explained: "Slaves make fire under the floor." Geron shook his head in disbelief. Virtus said: "Come on, I will show you!" They went down a flight of stairs. They came to one of the cellar rooms and there was a fire burning in an oven. A soot-covered slave was startled to see the boys. It was his job to keep the fire going. He bowed his head before the visitors. Virtus said: "This is our fire slave. He makes the floors warm and also the water for the bath. He has no chains on his ankles!"

Virtus led Geron back upstairs to the bathhouse. A servant had laid out clean clothes ready for them as Julia had instructed. There was a large sunken area in the room and warm water was flowing into it. It was steaming. Virtus took off his soldier's attire and let himself down into the water. He told Geron to do the same. It was so lusciously warm here!

Geron hesitated to get in so Virtus grabbed him and pulled him in. Two slaves approached. Geron watched as one of them went up to Virtus with a brush in his hand and began scrubbing. And, before he could react, the other slave had come up to him and began scrubbing as well. But the brush was soft, so Geron did not protest. The slave took something out of a small jar and rubbed it on Geron's hair and body. It was frothy. It smelled of flowers. They dunked under the water one more time and then a slave began to dry them off with a soft towel. Geron felt a little like a sissy and he thought: "Oh, these Romans!" After the bath a slave massaged oil into his skin.

Virtus said: "Your German clothes will be kept for your return home. But for now you will wear Roman clothes." Virtus had a blue tunic to put on and Geron got a red one. There were also short pants and a kind of mantle called a toga. A slave helped Geron to dress and even combed his hair which was painful. The same happened with Virtus so Geron did not complain.

He thought to himself: "What customs the Romans have! Suddenly Geron realized that there was something like transparent plates of ice over the light holes in the wall. He asked: "Why does the ice not melt there where the light comes in?"

Virtus explained: "That is a window, not ice. People made it." Geron went over to touch it. It really was not cold at all. And when he tapped on it, it made a pinging sound.

When the boys came out of the bath, Julia was waiting for them. She said enthusiastically: "How clean and handsome you are! Geron could stay here and be like our second son!" Virtus did not translate these words to Geron because he knew how much Geron loved his homeland. Julia continued talking to Virtus: "My dear son I am so thankful that the gods looked after you and led you back to us. I would like to go with you to the Temple of Mercury to offer a sacrifice and pray. I have arranged for servants to take me there. Please follow me."

Virtus explained: "We are going to the gods' house. Mother wants to pray. Father will be back later."

Geron asked: "Can one see the Roman gods? German gods are seen only by the Druids."

Virtus replied: "Come and see for yourself!"

Geron watched in amazement as Julia was seated in a chair attached to long poles and carried by four slaves. The boys followed after her. In the middle of the city, at the forum, they found themselves in a hive of people. The slaves put down the chair very softly at the bottom of the steps to the Mercury Temple. Julia asked the boys to walk on either side of her, and they climbed the steps together.

Geron admired the powerful columns which held up the roof. In the foyer there was a fire burning at an altar. White-robed priests were performing a sacrificial ceremony. Many people were kneeling in prayer. Julia pulled a small silk cushion out of her handbag and knelt on it. Geron knelt with Virtus at his side. Two priests began a song and a third priest tossed incense into the fire. Geron looked up shyly into the smoke to see if a god was visible. Tender music could be heard. The sacrifice was ended.

Julia walked with the boys into the inner temple. Virtus whispered: "Look, god Mercury!" When they entered Geron saw a tall, snow-white likeness of a man. He had small wings on his feet and a short staff in his hand with two snakes on it. Everything was carved from stone. Julia knelt down again and Virtus beside her.

But Geron took two steps backward and did not kneel. He thought: "How shall I pray to a naked man? My gods are honored by the sun, stars, lightning, thunder, rainbow, and wind." Suddenly he felt a tightness in his chest. He was happy to see Julia and Virtus stand up again. Julia had not noticed that Geron remained standing behind her while she was kneeling in silent prayer. But Virtus had an inkling of what Geron was thinking.

The slaves carried their mistress to the temple of the goddess Diana. At the bottom of the steps Julia purchased some ivy crowns and branches with red berries. She handed the greenery to the boys and went with them inside the small temple of the goddess. The goddess Diana was standing on a piece of rock in her snow-white beauty. An elk was standing at her side. Julia decorated the rock with the greenery. Again she knelt down with Virtus. Geron looked at the beautiful, tender face of the goddess and it reminded him of Helga when she had sung to the lamb. He closed his eyes and prayed in his soul: "Freya, protect me so that I may return home to the forests of Germany!"

Virtus and Julia stood up. The servants carried her back through the city. On the way they went through the street of the craftsmen. Geron got a look at the workshops of the blacksmiths, potters, boot makers, and cloth weavers. Virtus said: "Tomorrow we can visit the tradesmen."

Back at home Geron said: "I would like to go see my horse, Brenno, and give him feed and water myself." Virtus went with him to the stables. Brenno was resting in the straw next to the other horses. When he saw Geron he whinnied as if to say: "Ride me back to Germany!" Geron petted him and spoke gently to him. The stable boys had already given all the horses food and water. Geron said to Virtus: "There is good straw here. I could sleep here with Brenno."

Virtus laughed and said: "Here the straw is for slaves, not Geron. You will have your own room!" He went back to the house with his friend and showed Geron his bedroom. Some daylight was coming in through a hole covered in glass and illuminating the warm floor. Many thousands of little bits of stone formed figures of animals. Geron was afraid to step on them. Virtus pointed to a bed: "Here Geron, you can rest here until eating time. I will also rest." Geron sank down on the soft blanket and fell into a deep sleep.

The Return of Julus Severus

Julia had instructed the guards to let her know as soon as her husband, General Julus Severus, got home. She forbade any of the servants to mention to him that Virtus has returned. She had thought of a wonderful surprise. There was a festive table set in the dining room. There were many burning lights all around the room in such a number as normally reserved for highly festive occasions. In the late afternoon a messenger ran through the door and disappeared in the inner part of the house. He was bringing news of the master's return.

Julus Severus and his daughter, Claudia, climbed the marble steps to the villa. Julia met them. She was elaborately dressed. Julus greeted his wife with some wonderment and asked her: "Do we have important visitors? Is it an Imperial message from Rome?"

Julia answered with a smile: "You will soon find out. The table is already set. Yes, it is a fortunate message!" More curious than pleased, Julus allowed his wife to lead him and their daughter into the dining room. Yes, the room was beautifully decorated. It was hardly ever this festive. A servant brought a pitcher of warm water and a bowl for hand washing. Julia said: "While you are washing your hands, I will call the messenger."

Julus said to Claudia: "What is going on with Mother? I have not seen her this cheerful for over a year."

Claudia answered: "There must be two messengers. Look, the table is set for five."

A maid handed a towel to Julus. He could not resist asking her: "Who is here?" The servant shrugged her shoulders as if she did not know and quickly disappeared.

Father and daughter were alone in the room. They heard footsteps. Julia entered the room with a boy at her side. Claudia was the first to recognize him and screamed: "Virtus!" She ran to him and brother and sister gave each other a big hug.

Julus Severus stood there as if paralyzed. Inside he was bursting, but he was in the habit of maintaining his composure at all times. His only son, whom he believed dead, was alive and standing right here in front of him! Virtus ran to his father. Julus Severus did something he had not done in all the years of a hard soldier's life. He cried. Tears streamed down his cheeks as he whispered: "Virtus, my son!"

Julia said: "A German boy saved him and brought him here. Virtus was miserable as a captured slave."

Julus Severus asked: "Where is the German boy?"

Virtus answered: "I just looked in his room and he was sleeping. Come, let us go and get him. His name is Geron." He grabbed a light stand with oil lamps and walked ahead. When they arrived at Geron's room, he was lying on his back, sleeping. His blond hair was spread out on the red blanket like a golden halo around his head.

Claudia whispered: "How heavenly he looks!"

Mother said: "A wonderful boy brought back our Virtus to us. He is a precious boy, without guile." Geron opened his eyes in the flickering light but he was only half awake. He saw the light, Virtus, Julia, the dark-haired girl, and a tall Roman figure shimmering before him. Was he dreaming?

Virtus spoke softly to Geron: "Geron, Father is here with my sister, Claudia. Everyone wishes to thank you." Geron did not move but only gazed with his deep blue eyes into the distance. He was not yet fully awake. Julia bent down to him, stroked his hair, and kissed him on the forehead. Geron finally was awake. He was rather embarrassed and sat up. Virtus repeated what he had said to Geron. Geron shyly offered his handshake to Julus.

The general knew a few words of German. He hugged him as if he were his own son. He said: "I thank you, Geron. I thank you!" Claudia would have liked to also give Geron a hug, but, according to Roman custom, she merely bowed her head and smiled at him.

When all five were seated around the dining table, the servants were allowed to enter. There were more lamps put on the table and bowls of water for hand washing. Geron held his up to his mouth because he thought it was for drinking. The servant quickly took it away from his mouth with a shocked expression. Only then did Geron realize that the others were washing their hands in the bowls. Of course, everyone had noticed, but they just smiled and did not pay it any mind.

Soon everyone wanted to hear what the boys had to say about their experiences. Virtus began by telling his father all about his year in Germany. Geron did not understand one word, but he did notice when Claudia and her parents stopped eating and when the tone in Virtus' voice became subdued and sad. Father Julus had a deep frown on his forehead. Mother and daughter had tears in their eyes. Geron thought: "He must be telling them about his miserable existence as Wugo's slave." He also noticed a little later that the others sent friendly glances his way, and he noticed that Julus was nodding his head. Finally, everyone began eating again. Geron was offered a wide array of new foods and drinks. Everything tasted strange, but he liked it all.

After the meal everyone retired to the largest and most beautiful room in the house. There were paintings of the four seasons on the walls. The first time Geron saw this room, he thought the paintings were living people. He had never seen a wall mural before. Virtus explained in a few words that a man had painted the pictures on the wall with colored paints. In one corner there was a flickering fire that gave off no smoke. Everyone sat on a cushioned divan close to the fire. Virtus could not get enough of talking about his past year. Sometimes his father asked questions.

Suddenly Virtus turned to Geron and said: "My father says that you may remain here and live with us. You would be treated as my brother. You would learn our language and become a cavalry soldier with me. My father will give you silver. You can pay Wugo and then come back here and be a Roman, if you want."

Geron answered: "Virtus, you are happy here with your father and mother and your people. The Roman city is beautiful! I would love to look at everything. But my home is in Germany. Thank your father for me, that he wants to help me with Wugo." Virtus translated everything Geron had said. They all had a lively discussion about it.

Geron felt that he would like to leave the family to themselves for the evening. The rich food and wine had made him sleepy. Virtus brought him to his room. He said to Geron: "Claudia and I would like to have a brother. Father and Mother love you. You should think about it. Goodnight!" Virtus returned to his family and they talked until midnight.

Geron had trouble falling asleep. Everything he had seen today was another world! A foreign, beautiful, world. Brenno, his horse, could not go out on the meadow at night. He had to lie on the straw in the big, stone stable. The Roman priest had sacrificed to the white, stone-cold god. Evart had called out to the gods in lightning, thunder, wind, storm, and sun. Claudia, with the dark eyes, had given him a goodnight kiss on the cheek. Could she sing as nicely as Helga? He was sorry to disappoint Virtus. He had become such a good friend. But what about all the things Holger could tell him! His thoughts went back and forth.

When he finally relaxed enough to go to sleep, he had a dream. He was riding Brenno through the forests of home. Waldo was running next to him and barking joyously. The dream ended when Brenno jumped over a small stream. Geron fell into a deep sleep.

After midnight the Roman family went to their rooms. Virtus pushed aside the heavy curtain over Geron's door. He held up the oil lamp. Geron was sleeping peacefully. But what was that he was holding in his arms? Virtus tip-toed up to Geron's bed. It was his animal skin shirt. Geron had rolled it up and was holding it tightly. Virtus left the room quietly. "Tomorrow I will make sure that Geron has a wonderful day. Maybe he will decide to stay with us!"

With the Roman Craftsmen

The next morning Geron awoke on his bed. A beam of light was shining through a hole in the wall. It lit up a jumping elk on the floor that was not moving. Geron must try to grow accustomed to the fact that the Roman pictures were just representations of living things. He looked again at the elk. It must always stay at the same place.

Suddenly the door hanging was pushed aside. Virtus walked in and said with a merry voice: "Geron, get up and come with me!" He went up to Geron and jokingly pulled him out of bed. Geron did not really know how to dress himself correctly in the Roman clothes so Virtus helped him.

He led him down a hallway and then to some steps that led downward. That is where the bath room was located. They were met with warm steam. A slave bowed low in greeting to the young men. He carefully laid out clean clothes for them both on a stone bench. The floor was very warm and now Geron knew how the oven worked down below. The red ring marks from the iron cuffs on Virtus' feet were still noticeable. Virtus stepped into the bath which was an enormous basin of steaming water. He went under the water and blew air bubbles and waved for Geron to join him. Geron put his foot in the water to test the temperature.

Virtus sprang into action pulling Geron under the water. There began an animated splashing and dunking ending with both boys gasping and laughing. They sat on the steps of the bath and a slave walked up and handed Virtus a small jar with something in it that looked to Geron to be green and slimy. Geron thought: "It looks like vomit!" Virtus began to rub the mixture into his skin. The slave handed the jar to Geron but he waved it away. Virtus grabbed some and smeared it on Geron. It smelled very pleasant.

Virtus said: "With soap you can take away the dirt." Geron rubbed some on his face. Oh, how it burned his eyes! Virtus grabbed a towel from the slave, dunked it in the bath water, and washed the soap out of Geron's eyes. He explained: "Soap does not like the eyes. It burns." Virtus dried off Geron's face with the towel. His eyes were all bloodshot. Geron stayed sitting on the steps for a moment with closed eyes until the pain subsided.

When he finally opened his eyes Virtus was there with white hair. White froth was all over his body. He was rubbing his skin with a piece of cloth. He handed a cloth to Geron and showed him how one used the soap and washcloth to get clean. Geron thought: "Oh, these Romans!" But he let it go without saying anything. Virtus went back into the water and dunked his head. And the froth was gone. He looked to Geron like one of the Roman gods when he stepped out of the bath. Virtus said something to the slave and the slave rubbed some of the soap into Geron's hair, but he gave him the towel to cover his eyes.

Finally Geron was ready to rinse. The slave was drying off Virtus with a towel. When Geron stepped out of the bath a slave was waiting for him with a warmed towel. Geron suffered through being dried off like a small child would be in Germany.

Virtus walked up to him. He had a small, narrow-necked bottle in his hand and was shaking some of the contents onto his hands: Virtus declared: "Oleum! Good for the skin. Smells like flowers." It was true. When Geron sniffed the bottle he got a whiff of wonderful flower perfume. Virtus rubbed some of the oleum into his skin and shook some into Geron's hand as well. The slave came and rubbed some of the oil on their backs. Last of all, the slave combed their hair and handed them their clean clothes. The Roman bath was over.

Virtus said: "Now we will have breakfast and then visit the city."

Geron answered: "First I want to check on Brenno."

Virtus agreed: "Go to Brenno. I will eat and come after."

Geron walked into the stable and called Brenno. He nickered with happiness. But when Geron walked up to Brenno he did not rub Geron's shoulder with his head and nose as was his habit. Geron thought it must be because he smelled like a Roman. Brenno did not like that. Geron blew on his nose and rubbed his ears like he normally did and then the horse acted like his usual self again. Geron said to him: "This afternoon we will go for a ride!" A stable boy came and tossed some oats into the trough. Brenno ate it happily.

Geron climbed the steps to the villa. A servant appeared to escort him into the dining room. The whole family was seated and eating breakfast. Julia got up, walked to Geron, and said in German: "Good morning, dear Geron!" She had practiced this phrase with Virtus.

Geron said: "Good morning, Mother Julia!" She kissed him on both cheeks and led him to his place next to the master of the house.

Julus shook his hand: "Good morning, Geron!" Claudia gave him a friendly smile. The servant appeared with the washing bowl since Geron had been in the stable. This time he knew what to do with it. During the meal Virtus spoke to Geron: "Father gave me money to buy you something at the market. This morning we will visit the craft shops. In the afternoon Claudia and I would like to go horse riding with you!"

Geron thought: "This is going to be a wonderful day. And, I can ride Brenno again."

In the middle of breakfast Julus began to speak haltingly to Geron in German: "You, Geron are a good man, like my son! I send messenger to Wugo to bring him silver money. You may stay here and be Roman. You will have a good life." Geron was a little dismayed and he remained silent. Should he never return home? He felt that everyone here loved him because he had returned Virtus to them.

Virtus could sense the unrest that was coming over Geron. He said quickly: "Let us now go to the craft shops in the city. Just us two!"

Before they left the house a servant brought them each a red cloth and artfully arranged it over their shoulders. Geron felt strange with so much cloth wrapped around his body. But Virtus said: "Oh, Geron, you now a very handsome man! The Roman women will love you! I will go for a shave. The son of a general should not wear a beard."

Geron rubbed his chin on which the first hairs of a beard were beginning to show. He said: "I will not shave! I am a German!"

Virtus laughed: "Yes, yes, Geron, stay the way you are. Come on!"

The first stop was the barbershop. Geron watched as a man used a sharp knife to shave Virtus' beard and shorten his hair. He looked almost like a boy now. Suddenly Virtus laughed out loud. He said to Geron: "The man says he wants to buy your hair. He will make blond hair decorations out of it for Roman women. He offers much money. He believes you are my slave. He is disappointed that we are friends and he will not get blond hair." Geron's hair seemed even more golden since his Roman bath. The barber handed Virtus a shiny metal plate as a mirror. He nodded with satisfaction. He now looked like a real Roman. He handed the mirror to Geron. Geron saw his reflection in a mirror for the first time. He looked in his own eyes and believed himself to be looking into the eyes of his mother. He laughed and believed he saw the solid, white teeth of his father. The lips were just like his brother Gerwin's. His whole family was there! He looked long at his image.

Virtus asked: "You like you? Geron, you handsome man!" The barber tried once more to buy Geron's hair but Virtus just laughed and they left the shop.

They got to the street where all the craftsmen and tradespeople had their shops. They were met by the smell of freshly baked bread.

They were standing in front of a bakery. The baker was just taking a fresh loaf out of the oven with a wooden shovel. Slaves were turning large grinders to make the grain into flour. Virtus searched in his leather pouch. For a small coin he got two small, fresh loaves. They tasted delicious!

Further on they stopped in front of a lamp maker. A bellows was keeping the fire red hot. Next to it was an oven used to melt bronze. Some apprentices with blackened hands and faces were hammering and filing the metal after it had been poured and cooled. Virtus asked to look at a nice bronze lamp. A horse's head was molded on the handle. He gave it to Geron. Geron admired the fine horse's head while Virtus bargained with the artisan who made it. They came to an agreement. Virtus pulled a coin from his pouch and paid for the lamp. He said to Geron: "A gift for you!" Geron had never held something in hands that was so artistically made. Was it really for him? Virtus explained that it would be filled with oil at home. Then he could put the lamp in his room and the little horse's head would always shine. Geron was very happy to have it, even more because he thought it looked like Brenno.

Next they came to a shop where there were cooking pots boiling. Virtus said: "Here is where they make sapo that makes the eyes burn!" It was a soap shop. Steam and a sharp odor were coming from the pots. It reminded Geron of a witch's cauldron and a scary story that Gerwin had once told him. The soap maker handed Virtus and Geron small jars to smell. Geron noticed the same smell as in the bath this morning. Virtus explained: "When the soap is finished cooking, then flower perfume is put in."

They walked on and came to a very large shop. There was a man stomping his bare legs in a large bucket and his legs were fire-red. There were other buckets standing around with men stomping in them and their legs were green, or blue, or some other color. It was a dye shop. Woven cloth was put into the color buckets and a slave would stir them around with one leg until the cloth was evenly dyed. In the process all the slaves had thoroughly dyed skin on one leg. Others hung up the dyed cloth to dry. Geron now realized how the Romans got their clothes so colorful.

The boys came to a gold and coppersmith, a jewelry maker. Virtus said: "We should wear a sign of our friendship." He looked at copper armbands and chose two from the many displayed. Virtus said: "The rings are still open. The coppersmith will close them on our arms as a sign of our friendship." He pulled Geron into the shop. Virtus put the open copper ring around his wrist. Geron had to put the other ring on his wrist. Then the boys clasped hands and the coppersmith hammered the rings closed. They were now unable to remove them from their wrists.

Virtus counted out the number of coins the coppersmith asked as payment. He had now sealed his friendship with Geron according to Roman custom. Their friendship was now as strongly welded as the copper armbands. Virtus said: "Geron, let's visit the temple now. I would like to introduce you to Castor and Pollux. Geron had no idea what these names signified, but Virtus was his guide through this strange Roman world.

They wandered through the market. Geron noticed scantily dressed people at the top of a small hill. He asked Virtus: "Who are they?"

Virtus replied: "This is where slaves are bought and sold. It is the slave market." Geron looked at these people, how they were for sale like the horses and cattle next to them. Virtus added: "In our house the slaves have no cuffs or chains. Here also not. Slaves should have it good with us and like being house servants."

It was true. Geron had noticed that the slaves in Julus Severus's house were able to lead good lives. He had not seen a whip used nor heard any hateful words. But still, when he looked at the shy and somewhat anxious faces of these people up for sale, he felt sorry for them. What is a person who is not free, he thought.

Virtus walked further to a temple. There were marble statues in the foyer. No people were close to them. Virtus led Geron up to the twin statues of Castor and Pollux. He said: "These brothers have friendship in Heaven. We want to keep our friendship here on Earth." He took Geron's right hand and lay his other hand on the foot of the Castor statue. Then he told Geron: "Put your left hand on the foot of Pollux." Geron looked at Virtus to see if he was joking, but no, he was serious. He was quietly murmuring Latin words. Suddenly Virtus said out loud: "Now we will remain friends even after we have gone to our death!"

Geron felt that Virtus, a Roman, had a little of Holger's soul, Holger, his friend, who had learned so much from the Druids about life and death. When Virtus slowly removed his hand from the statue, Geron could see that he was emotional.

Virtus said: "Geron, I fear that you will go and I will never see you again! The gods sent you to me to set me free. I will never have another friend like you."

Geron tried to reassure Virtus: "Virtus, when I am back home you must come and visit me, and later I will visit you. You have sealed our friendship according to Roman custom and now I am sealing it in the way of the Germans." Geron took his knife out of his belt. He took the point and made a small puncture wound in Virtus' hand. Drops of blood welled up. He did the same to his own hand. Then he shook hands with Virtus.

Geron said: "Virtus, we will never forget each other. We are blood brothers now. Maybe sometime in the future your people and my people will be friends."

Silently they both descended the temple steps. Virtus knew in his heart that he should not try and talk Geron into staying here in Castra Vetera. He realized now that someone could be your friend even if you did not see them. He felt certain that Geron should return home to his life in Germany and he should stay here and lead his life as a Roman.

Three Take a Ride

Early in the afternoon three horses from Julus Severus' stable were standing ready. Two of the horses had saddles but the third had no saddle. Geron went up to Brenno. The stable boy asked Virtus if he was sure that the third horse should have no saddle. The German had taken it off. Virtus shook his head. He knew Geron wanted to ride in the German style.

Julia and Julus Severus were standing on the steps by the columns and waved when the two friends and Claudia rode by. Virtus explained to Geron that they were riding into the countryside to the house of his uncle, his father's brother Uncle Romanus was very rich. He had a large estate with herds of cattle and many horses. His uncle had not yet heard of Virtus' return. Virtus wanted to surprise him.

The horses walked slowly through the colorful hum of the city. Geron looked once again at the marketplace, the beautiful temple, and the palaces of the city. Yesterday he and Virtus had ridden through the north gate, but now they would leave the city by the south gate.

On the way they met farmers with horses and carts. They were bringing vegetables, fruit, and meat to the market.

The road was paved with stones but beside it there was a riding path. The horses were able to go faster on this path. Virtus rode in front. He brought his horse to a gallop. Claudia was immediately behind Virtus, and Geron brought up the rear. When the path became a little steep they walked their horses. Then Claudia would ride next to Geron. Since she could not speak Geron's language, she had made up a word game. (She had learned three words of German from Virtus.) She would point to something and ask: "How say German?"

Geron would answer in German, "Horse," for example. She pointed to the mane, the ears, the neck, and the teeth. Geron would say the words in German and Claudia would try and repeat them. She had an especially difficult time pronouncing the word, "Pferdeschwanz" (horse's tail). Claudia laughed loudly.

After a while they noticed low buildings not far from the riding path. Smoke was rising from these buildings. Geron asked what they were.

Virtus replied: "There is made *tegula* for building houses and roof. Let's go watch." He went in the direction of the brick-making operation. Many workers were forming rectangular bricks out of clay. Others would stack them under open-sided shelters where they could dry. Virtus spoke with a foreman and explained that they wished to watch the brick-making. When they got to the place where the smoke was pouring out, Geron stared in amazement. Large ovens were in operation. Some were being heated. Dried clay bricks were put into others. People were hauling finished, hard, red-brown bricks out of one oven that was almost cool. A large number of workers were present. It reminded Geron of an anthill. Now Geron knew how the Romans got all of those red bricks. The tiles for roofs were made from flat pieces of clay. There were enormous piles of wood to heat the ovens that would harden the clay. Geron suddenly remembered how his father had gathered rushes at the lake for their new roof, and how he and Gerwin had bundled them.

The three were once again sitting on their horses, riding along harvested fields. Claudia suggested they have a little race. Her father had given her a young, fast horse. They lined up their horses at the end of a field. A far-off tree on the top of a hill was to be the finish line. The Roman horses were more used to setting off at a command, so Geron was a little behind at first. But he talked to Brenno and whistled softly in the horse's ear. Suddenly they came to a rocky area. The Roman horses slowed a little. Brenno shot over the rocks like an arrow. When they reached soft earth again, the Roman horses moved to the front. Soon it looked as if all three horses would finish at the same time, they were so close together. When they finally reached the finish line tree, no one could tell who the front runner was. Geron admired Claudia for her ability as a rider. She was, after all, a whole year younger than he.

They stopped at a stream to rest and let the horses drink. Virtus said: "It's not much farther to the fields belonging to Uncle Romanus." From then on they rode at a more leisurely pace. In the distance could be seen large farm buildings and a beautifully constructed villa. There was a large herd of cattle grazing by the outbuildings. There was a special fenced pasture in which grazed many red-brown and black horses. Geron thought of their five cows, two horses, and a few sheep at home. That was the extent of their holdings.

Virtus remarked: "All the animals and slaves that you see belong to Uncle Romanus. Two of his sons were soldiers. They were killed in the Gallia war. Romanus lives alone now with his wife and all his riches. He is my father's older brother." After the death of his own sons, Romanus had turned all of his love to Virtus and named him as his heir. And then, Virtus was also taken by the Germans and believed to have been killed. So, Romanus now not only lived in mourning for his two sons, but also for his nephew, Virtus.

From the villa which stood on a hill there was a view of the entire surroundings. Romanus had observed the three riders as they approached. He went from the terrace into the courtyard. The first person he recognized was Claudia who had just visited a few days earlier with her father. But who were these two young men she had brought with her? Virtus had already jumped off his horse and was running toward his uncle. Claudia also dismounted. Geron was a little shy and remained seated on his horse. He heard Romanus let out a cry of happiness and he saw him hugging Virtus. Just as the homecoming with Virtus's father had been, there were joyful tears and laughter. Geron slid from his horse. Yes, now he was once again assured that his idea to free Virtus from Wugo's chains had not been a mistake. How much happiness had already come from breaking those chains by the hearth fire in the old house!

When Romanus' wife heard all the commotion, she came hurrying out of the house. The happy greetings continued. While Virtus was quickly explaining his fate as a slave, Geron waited. Virtus suddenly ran up to him and took him to introduce to Romanus. Brenno walked along with them. Romanus clapped Geron on the shoulder and started talking to him. He did not seem to mind that the German boy did not understand one word of his praise and thanks. Virtus let him talk and then explained that Geron did not understand Latin.

Stable boys came and took the horses away to the stable. The guests were invited up to the terrace. Geron asked Virtus: "May I go to the horse pasture while you talk to your uncle? The horses are fantastic!" Geron would rather do that than listen to long conversations in Latin. Virtus explained to his uncle what Geron wished to do. Geron was asked to stay for a short toast of welcome, naturally with "sour water," and then he was free to go.

Geron climbed the wooden fence surrounding the horse pasture. There must have been about thirty horses grazing there. They were well looked after. Geron could tell because they were not shy and allowed him to touch them with his hand. A beautiful reddish-brown stallion was especially friendly. He was a young animal. The horse must have noticed that there was some Roman rice bread in Geron's leather pouch. Geron opened the pouch and fed the stallion all of the bread down to the last crumb. He quickly decided to call the horse "Fire Fox." Fire Fox followed Geron and nudged his shoulder, trying to get Geron to pet him some more.

Geron had the thought that perhaps Fire Fox would allow him to ride him. He was used to going for short rides on Brenno without reins. He jumped up on the horse's back. Fire Fox just stood there for a moment. Geron patted his mane and neck. Then Geron tried giving him a slight nudge in the ribs and whistled softly in his ear. He started walking a few steps. Then he shot his head up and broke into a gallop. Geron had enough presence of mind to match his own movements with those of the horse and hold fast with his legs.

It was going wonderfully but Geron did not know how he would bring Fire Fox to a halt. It did not help to command: "Halt!" Then he had an idea. He scooted his hands along the horse's neck, over his ears, and covered the horse's eyes with the palms of his hands. The horse began to slow down and eventually stopped. Geron thought he would like to try that again right away. He brought Fire Fox to a gallop again and was again able to stop him. Geron forgot the time. After he had played this game at least a dozen times, he noticed that Fire Fox would stop as soon as Geron started going along his neck with his hands. He no longer needed to cover the horse's eyes. What an intelligent horse!

Geron heard his name being called while he was in the middle of one of these practice rides. It was Virtus. He was walking to the horse pasture with Romanus and Claudia. Geron brought Fire Fox to a standstill. He jumped off the horse feeling a little guilty and walked toward the others with some hesitation. He jumped over the fence and noticed that Fire Fox followed him. Romanus, Virtus, and Claudia were very enthusiastic about how Geron could ride without reins or saddle.

As Romanus had heard so many good things about Geron from Virtus, he said: "Tell your friend I am giving him a horse since he has brought you back to me. He may choose one and take it back to Germany with him." Virtus told Geron what his uncle had said.

At first, Geron could not believe that someone would give another person a horse, just like that. When he finally understood that this was really Romanus' wish, he pointed to Fire Fox who was still waiting by the fence. He had only one concern. How would he get along with Brenno?

He quietly asked Virtus how one said "Thank you" in Latin. He went to Romanus, grabbed his right hand, gave it a hearty shake, and said: "Gratias, gratias, gratias!" Geron had spoken Latin for the first time in his life in thanks for Fire Fox.

Romanus was so happy about the return of his nephew, Virtus, that he said: "You three young people will be our guests tonight. I will send someone to Castra Vetera to tell them you will not be back until tomorrow." Everyone agreed.

Geron thought at once: "I can try out riding with Brenno and Fire Fox together." In the courtyard Romanus told his horse master to send a fast rider to the house of Julus Severus in Castra Vetera. He also told him to help Geron with the new horse. He must learn to ride with the two horses together. Romanus left Geron with the horse master and went back to the house with the others.

The horse master had been a show rider in a circus. He was not only good with horses, but also with people. He was friendly with Geron right away. Brenno and Fire Fox must first learn to eat oats out of the same bucket. Afterward they could begin with the riding practice. The horses were tied together. Geron rode on Brenno and Fire Fox trotted next to him. The horse master saw how talented Geron was with horses. He showed Geron how the circus riders jump from one horse to the other. Geron tried it and was successful. That was such great fun.

Night was approaching and it was time to stop the riding practice. The blond riding artist was thoroughly soaked with sweat. When he got back to the villa, he was ordered into the Roman bath immediately. And this time it went without eyes burning from soap suds.

It was a happy circle of people who gathered around the open fire that evening in the warm living room. Hanging on long chains from the ceiling were lamps that gave off soft, glowing light. The three young guests and their hosts were lounging on the soft cushions. Geron was seated between Virtus and Claudia.

Romanus had a young Greek slave. She had a wonderful singing voice and played the lyre in accompaniment. She had been brought here to the North from warm, sunny Greece. When she sang her Greek songs she was seized by homesickness for the blue shores and white temples of her homeland. She wore a snow-white, Greek robe with finely embroidered trim.

Geron was under the spell of her beauty and the music. It was the same when Helga sang in the sheep pasture. Helga would be petting a lamb she held on her lap. The Greek girl was bringing forth gentle tones from the strings of her lyre. She sang about the gods of Greece and the hero, Achilles.

To Geron it was music without words since she was singing in Greek. But his heart was opened by the music. He thought: "The Greeks must also have had a god-singer among them who brought them the songs from the Greek Valhalla."

Suddenly Geron realized that during the singing Claudia had put her head on his shoulder and laid her hand on his. Claudia had learned a few more words of German from her brother. When the song was finished she whispered to Geron: "I love Geron-brother!" Geron was surprised that a proud and rich Roman girl could like a strange, poor German. Claudia thought to herself: "I know he is going away from here to Germany into the dark forests. But every day that he is still here shall be a day of friendship!"

Servants brought wine in cups and very fine honey cakes. The Greek girl sang again. The warmth, the wine, and the soft cushions had their effect. In the middle of the song Geron fell asleep. Of course, that amused the Romans, but the concert continued with one sleeping guest.

Geron awoke at a late hour when the lights were being extinguished. He had come out of a beautiful dream. The music had given him wonderful pictures. Virtus spoke to him: "Geron, get up! It's time for bed!"

The Trip on the Rhine

Two days later at breakfast, Julus Severus declared: "Tomorrow I have a surprise for everyone. I have ordered a boat with six rowers. You are all invited for a boat ride on the Rhine. We will visit the next Roman city upstream called Novaesium." Novaesium was the home base for a legion. The general wished to discuss some plans with the commanders there. Julus spoke further: "It is a large, comfortable boat. The trip takes a good half-day. We will stay the night in a tavern in Novaesium. While I am meeting with the commanders you may look around the city with Geron." Everyone, including Geron, was looking forward to this trip. A servant would go along to take care of food and drink.

Julus Severus had ordered a military boat with oars. To reach the Rhine they had to ride a good distance on horseback. Geron suggested he leave Brenno in the stable and ride Fire Fox. He did not want Brenno to have to bear a Roman saddle on the ride back from the river with a Roman stable boy on his back.

Everyone arose very early the next morning. Everything had been prepared. When Geron saw the boat he thought: "That boat is at least five times as long as I am!" In the very back there was a small awning to protect the passengers from sun and rain. The six rowers sat in the middle and to the front on benches, two together and one oar per man. A seventh man was at the helm. Julus Severus wore his general's uniform. He looked splendid in his gold-plated breastplate. Geron watched in amazement as the six rowers struck out in rhythm to quickly move the boat forward once it was in the water. The boat went very fast since the oars were very long. They met other boats on the river from time to time. There were stretches of a road on the left bank where riders, wanderers, and carts could be seen.

It was afternoon when the boat landed at Novaesium. There was a ways to go by horse because the Romans did not build their cities very close to the river banks because of the danger of flooding.

In the middle of the city there was a nice tavern for important people. A messenger had been sent the day before to tell of the general's impending arrival. Everything was prepared to receive his family. Julus Severus soon took leave of the others to attend his meeting. After a short rest and refreshment, Julia, her children, and Geron went to have a look at the city. The most interesting feature was the market. It was almost as large as the one in Castra Vetera.

Julia and Claudia made some purchases. Geron saw there was a cattle market and next to it a slave market just like in Castra Vetera. He went up to it and noticed among the slaves displayed for sale a blond German youth, still a boy, really. He was wearing a light robe and was freezing cold because of his uncovered legs. Geron went up to him and spoke: "Where are you from?"

The boy was startled when he realized someone was speaking to him in his own language. He looked up and saw Geron. Somewhat shyly, he answered: "I come from the Lupia area, as the Romans say."

Geron inquired further: "Why are you here and what is your name?"

The boy replied: "My name is Sigbert. I went too far downriver while fishing. Roman soldiers caught me and sold me to this market. Are you also a slave?"

Geron quickly replied: "No. But tell me, from which family are you?"

Sigbert answered: "I come from the Sigmann family. I am the only son and have two sisters. They do not know what terrible fate has befallen me. Fellow German, can you not buy me?" He looked at Geron with pleading in his eyes.

Virtus had just walked up and heard the boy's last words. Geron was upset at the fate of this German brother. He said to Virtus: "Virtus, if I gave my horse, Fire Fox, could I exchange him for this slave?"

Virtus answered: "A horse is not enough. I would think it would take two horses. But what do you want with a slave?"

Geron replied: "I want to give him his freedom and return him to his homeland, just as I did with you."

Virtus was surprised. He was silent for some time and thought about this. He looked at the blond slave and back at Geron. Finally he said: "Fire Fox is not enough. I will speak with Mother. I am going to get her now."

Since the slave handler was busy with another transaction Geron had time to speak more with Sigbert. He asked him: "How long have you been in captivity?"

Sigbert replied: "One month it must be. At first I had to work with some soldiers in a castle. That was not bad. Then the slave trader bought me. He always beats me for small transgressions. My parents do not know why I disappeared, whether I drowned or was killed. Maybe you could bring them news of me."

Geron thought for a moment if he should also give Brenno and go back home with Sigbert on foot. Julia and Claudia were close by at a fabric stand. Virtus found them there and brought them both to the slave market. He quickly told them that Geron wished to give his horse, Fire Fox, as price for a German slave. They had an animated discussion among themselves about this surprising turn of events.

Julia went to where Geron was waiting and the slave trader came up to them. There had not been much interest today for the somewhat young and weak German boy. Julia asked about the price. The trader gave her a figure that was a little lower than the day before. Virtus got involved and began to bargain. Suddenly Geron saw the trader give Virtus a handshake. The slave had been purchased! But the trader wanted to see money right now. Julia said: "My son is going now to get it from my husband. Our German will wait here."

Virtus explained to Geron: "We have purchased the slave for you. I will go to Father now and hope that he is in agreement. You wait here."

What a joy it was for Geron to be able to hear and speak German again! He began to tell Sigbert all the things he had experienced with Virtus and why he had come to Roman territory.

Sigbert was still in disbelief that he may have been purchased and would be going back with Geron to his home. They awaited Virtus' return with great tension. He came with his father. Geron could see from the look on Virtus' face that it was good news. When the slave trader saw the great general approaching he practically jumped from the ground. He could have asked more for the slave!

Julus said to Geron: "You have given me back my son, so I am giving you the German!" He opened the bulging leather pouch on his belt and counted out the agreed upon number of gold pieces into the waiting hand of the slave trader.

Geron was so surprised by the speed of events that he could only grasp the general's hand and stammer: "Thank you, Father Julus!"

The general grabbed a hand full of hair on the German slave's head and, in a friendly manner, pointing to Geron, said: "This is your master!" The boy finally understood what had happened. He broke out in tears and hugged Geron.

Geron said gently: "Sigbert, be brave! Don't cry!" The boy dried his eyes with the corner of Geron's shoulder cloth and stood erect.

The next day the six-oared boat was once again making its way down the Rhine, but this time there was an extra passenger, Sigbert. After a few hours of travel Virtus became bored. He said: "Geron, shall we both row for a while?" They sat on the front rowing bench and relieved two soldiers. Virtus was familiar with rowing. But Geron made a big splash with the oar at first and hit the oar of the man behind him. A soldier helped him master the oar until he got into the rhythm of it. Soon he was rowing like an old hand.

The Return to Germany

Geron had asked Virtus if he would speak to his father about Geron's returning home three days from now. Virtus knew that it had to happen even though it was so very hard for him to see his beloved friend leave. Geron wanted to give Julus his horse, Fire Fox, as payment for the German slave. But Julus declared: "When I give a gift, it stays a gift!" And that is how it stayed.

Virtus had one worry and that was that the two young Germans could be captured again on the way home. His father said: "I will write a free pass for them on a wax tablet and imprint it with my seal. That will be sufficient anywhere in Roman territory for them to pass through unharmed." He also gave Geron a bag of silver as ransom money to give to Wugo. On top of that, he gave Geron some traveling money.

The morning of their departure arrived. Geron had laid out his sheepskin clothing and his weapons the night before. Julia had insisted on one thing and that was that he and Sigbert put on the leather pants she had purchased for them so they would not freeze in the winter cold on the long trip home. After he was dressed he took the bear teeth necklace in his hand. He had the impression that he could hear the rustling of the trees in the forests of Germany. He closed his eyes and pressed the necklace to his face with both hands. He did not notice that the door curtain to his room had been raised.

It was Claudia. She walked quietly up to Geron and lay both her hands on his shoulders. Geron slowly let the necklace fall from his face. He looked into Claudia's dark, sad eyes. She hugged his neck and whispered words she had learned from Virtus: "Geron, I will never forget you!" And then she kissed him goodbye. She took something hard and metallic out of a little purse tied to her belt. She took the copper armband on Geron's wrist and scratched a little cross into the copper metal.

He spoke to her: "Geron will never forget Claudia!" He tore one of the bear teeth from his necklace, plucked a hair from his head, and wrapped it around the tooth. He put it in Claudia's hand. But he put the necklace back in his pocket.

It had been decided that Virtus and Claudia would accompany the two German boys to the Rhine River. There were four horses ready and waiting in the courtyard below. Sigbert would be able to ride Fire Fox. He had a rucksack packed full of provisions for the long trip. Geron said goodbye to Julia and Julus Severus in the foyer. Virtus said to Geron: "Mother Julia is giving this to you to take to Mother Ina."

Julia loosened a finely wrought gold chain from her neck and put it into Geron's hand. She had also learned a few words from Virtus. She hugged Geron and said: "Geron, come again!" She wrapped the jewelry in a fine linen cloth and put both in a leather pouch. Geron put the gift in his sheepskin pouch. He had also carefully packed away the oil lamp and a small container of oil.

Julus handed him a new and wonderful Roman ax and said: "Here, Geron, for your father!" Then he hugged the boy to him with great force and said: "My heartfelt thanks! You brought me Virtus! My life is full of joy again!"

The four young people mounted their horses in the courtyard. From all sides the servants appeared from behind columns and walls to wave goodbye. They all had come to love Geron, and it was nicer for them to serve in a happy household than a mournful one.

The old watchman was standing at the gate. He walked up and handed Geron a pair of Roman leather gloves for the coming winter cold. His face was glowing. They rode through a forum in the city and Virtus pointed up to a temple and said: "Castor and Pollux. We will never forget!"

They were nearing the bridge over the Rhine. Virtus said: "We will ride with you over the bridge to the first hill! Geron, you ride in front. We want to see what the guards at the bridge say." Geron and Sigbert rode at the fore. The bridge guards skeptically stepped forward to halt the riders. Geron showed them the wax tablet. They looked and read. Opened mouthed, they let the two pass. Virtus and Claudia followed.

Geron said to Virtus: "Your father is a great magician." They both laughed.

They had now reached the hill where goodbyes must be said. They all dismounted. Sigbert wanted to thank Virtus once again, but Virtus said: "Thank Geron."

Geron walked to Claudia and she gave him a huge smile that he could remember always with happiness. He cupped his hands for her to use as a step up to remount her horse. Geron and Virtus now said their goodbyes and they both found this very strange. Suddenly, Virtus grabbed the copper bracelet on Geron's arm and said: "Castor!"

Geron did likewise and answered: "Pollux!" They were the only ones who knew the significance of these words. Geron swung himself onto his horse. Virtus pressed his cheek to Brenno's nose and whispered: "Brenno, good Brenno. You carried me into freedom."

Geron called out: "Hali," as Brenno and Fire Fox trotted off. Behind him he could hear a long, drawn-out "Haloh!" Sigbert and Geron galloped down the hill toward the forest and the road home. Geron stopped once and looked back. Brother and sister were still on the hilltop. One last wave and then the two boys turned toward the forest shadows.

Up the Lupia River

It was as if Brenno sensed that he was returning to his German home. He needed no encouragement and Fire Fox did a good job of keeping up with him. After a few hours they came to the Lupia River. There they rested the horses and let them drink. They went by way of the Roman road which went upriver. A troop of soldiers with an officer came riding from the opposite direction. The soldiers barred their way and were talking excitedly among themselves. Geron noticed that they were acting as if they may attack at any moment. He fearlessly went to the officer and handed him the wax tablet from Julus Severus.

The officer began to read. His eyes became wide and he gave his soldiers a command. Geron could hear the name "Julus Severus." The soldiers allowed them to pass. The commander returned the wax tablet to Geron and actually saluted him. Geron said: "Gratias," to give the impression that he could speak Latin.

After they had ridden a little further, Sigbert said: "Geron, they really had respect for you. That is a precious tablet with the Roman magic on it!" In the evening they came to a tavern. Sigbert suggested: "Would we not be better off to ride further and spend the night in the forest? I'm scared to be with more Romans."

Geron replied: "I am not afraid. The night will be cold. I have Roman money with me." They tied the horses under a protective roof and walked inside. There were only a few travelers there. When they appeared in the tavern the guests gave them suspicious looks. Geron walked up to the innkeeper who was ready to show both of them the door. Geron said: "Salve!" He put the tablet in front of the innkeeper's nose. He thought it was fun to work a little Roman magic. The innkeeper looked at the tablet but, unfortunately, he could not read. But he did recognize the seal.

One of the guests could read quite well and read the tablet aloud within hearing range of all the others. The innkeeper bowed to Geron and asked him in broken German: "What you wish, sir? Warm soup and overnight, oats for horses?" The innkeeper led them to a place at the table and soon bowls of steaming soup were put before them. They also ate some of the provisions from Sigbert's rucksack.

The next morning when it was time to pay, Geron said: "Write it down!" Virtus had taught him the Roman numbers up to one hundred. The innkeeper thought that he should probably not charge more than a soldier's rate for someone protected by a general. So he wrote "XXX," and Geron paid with the appropriate silver coin. Soon the two youths were riding down the road again.

The next evening there was a horse trader in the tavern who wanted to buy Fire Fox from Geron. He offered to pay in gold. But Geron would not sell him.

Julus Severus had asked Geron to give the commander at the Castle Arbalo a little wax tablet. It was getting toward evening when they arrived there. Sigbert said: "This is where they brought me after I was captured. I worked in the kitchen until I was sold to the slave trader. Geron, I am worried someone will capture me again while we are there."

Geron felt confident and he said: "Trust me! As long as you are with me, the Romans will leave you alone." The two Germans neared the castle gates. The guards' eyes narrowed in suspicion. The beautiful horses caught their eyes. But when the two dismounted from their horses, one of the guards said: "Hey, I know them! One was with the son of Julus Severus, and the other was here as a kitchen helper." Geron was greeted in a friendly manner.

He said: "Salute! Gaius!" Without having to show the wax tablet they were led into the large courtyard and their presence immediately reported to Gaius. Geron was told to report to Gaius. Sigbert was to stay below with the horses. Geron took the message from Castra Vetera from his pocket and handed it to Gaius. Virtus had explained to him that the message contained greetings, thanks, and an accounting of the horse that had been loaned to Virtus. Gaius called for an interpreter, a German who had joined the Roman military. Geron was able to fully detail how everything had happened with the return of Virtus to his father's home. It was no wonder that Gaius offered them both food and lodging for themselves and their horses that night.

Geron returned to the courtyard to find Sigbert in trouble. It was believed that he had escaped from the slave trader who bought him. There was a lively discussion taking place and they had already bound Sigbert's hands behind his back. Geron asked the interpreter to come to his assistance. The incident was soon cleared up. Geron untied Sigbert's hands. Sigbert wanted to ride away from there immediately. Geron calmed him: "We have been invited to stay the night here. The men had no way of knowing what had happened."

When it was time to go to bed, the two lay side by side in the straw in a clean, little room where Roman officers were also quartered. Sigbert said quietly to Geron: "I don't know how I will ever thank you, Geron. We are poor. We have only three cows and some sheep. My father is a good hunter, but he has only one horse. Maybe I can do some work for you sometime; a year, or even longer, if you want. According to Roman law I would have to work for you my whole life! I would like to be your servant. You are so courageous and have a good heart. How shall I thank you?"

Geron replied: "Sigbert, the gods and the Norns guide our destiny. They led me to you. I was given the opportunity to help you. Someday I may be happy to be able to ask for your help. But right now, tell me, where is the way to your father's house from the Lupia?"

Sigbert answered: "When we get to the source we ride on the left-hand path. It's about one hour's ride from there."

And Geron went on: "And I must ride on the right-hand path for half a day. But before, I will bring you back to your father."

Sigbert could not sleep for a long time. The shock of being tied up again was still trembling through his limbs. He listened to the deep, regular breathing of Geron. That brought some quiet to him and the thought of being so close to his home also helped take him into peaceful sleep.

The Homecoming

Sigbert and Geron reached the source spring of the Lupia after a two day's ride. It was foggy and cold. The first snowflakes were falling. Horses and riders quenched their thirst. Geron sat by the spring and thought back on how he and Virtus had rested here on their first day after their flight. Virtus had splashed his hands in the water and said: "Lupia water flows to Castra Vetera and the house of my father!" How much had happened in the weeks since that day! He felt as if he were a different person. He looked at the copper bracelet on his arm. The metal was cold. Did not a part of him remain in Castra Vetera? He closed his eyes. He could see the images in his mind's eye: Virtus, Claudia, Julia, Julus Severus, Castor, Pollux, the Greek singer.

Geron had forgotten his surroundings and was startled when Sigbert asked: "Shall we go? I'm anxious to get home!"

Geron splashed his hands in the water: "Yes, I'm coming!" He found a golden autumn leaf under the thickening layer of snow and tossed it into the flowing river. Sigbert was already on his horse. Geron looked a long time at the leaf disappearing down the Lupia. He took out the bear teeth necklace and hung it around his neck. He got on Brenno and asked Sigbert: "Do you have dogs?"

Sigbert replied: "Yes, a hunting dog. But he is not dangerous. He won't hurt the horses."

Geron was silent for the rest of the ride and let Sigbert ride ahead. There was still a light snow falling. All at once a small valley opened in front of them. A humble little house was perched on a ledge. Sigbert yelped for joy: "There it is!" He had to hold himself back from riding away from Geron. Nobody was outside. A thin trail of smoke was coming from the roof. The two rode down the middle of the meadow toward the house. Geron held Brenno back a little. Sigbert pushed forward. Suddenly a dog barked loudly and sprang from underneath the skins covering the door opening. Sigbert called out the dog's name and jumped off his horse. Two girls hurried out of the house, then the mother and father.

Geron halted his horse and looked out over the white landscape. He did not want to interfere with the homecoming. The girls were shouting, laughing, and crying. Geron slowly went up to the house. Sigbert tore himself from his mother's arms and hurried to meet him. With a few words, the parents were clear about how grateful they were to Geron. They all entered the house.

Geron felt at home again. There it was, the stillness, the hearth with the flickering fire, the three cows off to one side of the house, contentedly chewing their cud, a newborn calf by their side, the meat being smoked in the rafters, the weaving loom in one corner, the sheep's wool to be spun by the girls, and the carving bench of the father. Someone added wood to the fire to give more light.

Now it was time to hear all the stories! Sigbert's father, Sigmann, reported about a Druid Gathering two weeks ago. He had heard talk about a Roman slave being taken by a young German. There were a lot of hard feelings between the people involved. The father of the kidnapper was asked to pay a fine since no one knew if his son would ever return. The man making the complaint against him was not there because he was very ill. Geron admitted that he was the guilty party and said he was the son of German. He said: "I will pay the fine to the complainant!"

They ate meat from the spit and drank fresh milk from a mug that was passed around. Geron explained: "It is now late afternoon. I would like to leave now for home and my family. We will see each other again soon!" Even though they begged him to stay the night, Geron remained steadfast in his desire to take his leave.

Sigbert whispered: "I remain your servant!"

Geron replied: "My friend!"

Sigbert helped Geron get Brenno and Fire Fox set for the ride home. Geron returned to the source spring. Strangely enough, he did not feel the need to hurry. It would be late at night anyway when he arrived home.

It was already dusk by the time he arrived at the spring. He gave one last look to the flowing water and then he started for home. As long as the waning light was still shining it was easy to find his way through the forest and meadows. But when darkness fell Geron lost his way on the snow-covered path and was riding aimlessly through the woods. Sometimes he would find himself in thick underbrush and would have to turn back. Finally he let the reins go so Brenno could find his own way. It had stopped snowing. Slowly Geron began to sense a familiarity with his surroundings. Brenno had found the path again.

It must have been close to midnight when the fields of his home appeared before him, then the old house, the new house, the stream, and the linden tree. Inside the house everyone was deeply asleep. Should he make any noise? Should he awaken them? No. He could sleep in the old house with the animals and not bother anyone. If he rode up against the wind even Waldo would not notice anything.

He rode to the old house and got off his horse. Everything was quiet. Inside the house a smoky warmth permeated the air. The cows were asleep on one half of the floor and on the other half, Father's horse. Geron built up the fire to give light. The door opening was just high enough so the horses could get through if they lowered their heads. He directed them inside and showed them the straw for their beds. He hung the weapons back up on the wall and put the ax and his leather pouch in the old trunk. He looked for the iron chains that he had put inside but they were gone.

Geron sat for a while by the fire to warm himself. He remembered how Virtus had sat there while Geron worked on breaking the chains on his legs. And now, everything was all right again! Or, was it? Father would understand, but what about Wugo? As he held his hands over the coals he murmured: "Norns, helpers of our destiny, I give you thanks!" He found a place in the straw between the horses, his loyal companions, who had done such a wonderful job of carrying him and Sigbert back to their homeland. He petted each of them on the neck and mane and whispered some words of thanks to them. And why not? Why should the animals not be thanked for their service? Then Geron sank into a deep sleep.

In the early morning hours when it was still dark outside, German got up to see what the weather was like. He was planning to go hunting in the forest. The stars were still out. He said to himself: "I can look about the fire in the old house and then go with Waldo for a morning hunt."

He walked to the old house in the dawn light and was going to remove the wood from in front of the door but it was already laid to one side. He thought that was strange since he was sure he had put it in front of the door the night before. He walked inside the dark room to the fire, blew on the coals, and added some kindling wood. The horses and rider were still sleeping soundly after the tiring ride of the night before.

German thought it odd that there was a stronger odor of horses in the house than normal. German's eyes slowly became used to the dark and he looked around. He started. There were three horses lying in the straw! And between the horses – was that a stranger who had spent the night here without asking? He put another handful of wood shavings in the fire. Yes, there was only one rider sleeping between the two horses. Was that not . . . Geron? German's throat got tight and his eyes filled with tears. He walked a few steps toward Geron and knelt down. Yes, it was Geron, his son! He ran a hand over Geron's hair. When he could talk, he whispered: "Geron, my dear Geron!"

The sleeping youth opened his eyes. In the reddish light of the fire he saw his father leaning over him. He slowly raised his arms and hugged his father's head. Geron's voice whispered a plea: "Father, please don't be angry with me!" The tears bespoke German's true feelings and there was no anger in them. Although the two never spoke of it again, they both knew that their bond was stronger than ever.

A little while later German put some dry wood on the fire so that it would be lighter inside. The two stallions had also arisen. German looked at Fire Fox with a practiced eye. He said: "What a beautiful horse! To whom does he belong?"

Geron replied happily: "Us, father, he belongs to us! He is one of the gifts that I was given for bringing Virtus back to his home. And for Wugo I have silver money."

Father got a serious look on his face and said: "Wugo does not need any silver now. A week ago his injured leg finally got the best of him and he died. He went into the great unknown in a firestorm of pain." Geron was silent. He sat down by the fire was lost in his thoughts.

After a few minutes passed, German said: "Life goes on! Come on, let's bring some happiness to the new house." German put his arm around Geron's shoulder as they walked to the house. The stars had begun to fade. Geron looked up toward the west and saw the twin stars, Castor and Pollux. But German was pulling him forward. There was a loud bark heard coming from the house. Waldo ran wildly toward Geron and jumped on him and was beside himself with overflowing joy. Father hurried inside and called: "Geron is here! Geron has returned!"

There had never been such an uproar in the new house. Gerda, Gerwin, Ina, and Uralda ran out the door. Geron was almost overcome by the intensity of their greeting, such complete joy and happiness.

There was a long breakfast in German's house that morning and a long period of storytelling. Afterward, the two horses were brought from their stable in the old house. Fire Fox was greatly admired by all. Gerwin said: "Geron, since you have Fire Fox, now Gerda and I could ride Brenno!"

But Geron replied: "No, Brenno is my horse and he will always be my horse. But if you are good to him, I will teach you both to ride Fire Fox."

They went back to the warmth of the new house. Geron asked Gerwin to go to the old house and get his leather pouch and the ax in the old trunk. He said to his mother and father: "Virtus' parents gave me gifts to give to you. They thought you must have had much worry because of their son and because I freed him and returned him to his family." Geron did not spoil the surprise by telling them what the gifts were. When Gerwin returned Geron took the ax from him and said: "Here, Father! This is your Roman ax that Julus Severus sends with his thanks."

German took the ax in his hands and said: "A wonderful ax! We could build another house with this!"

Geron felt around in his leather pouch and brought out a white linen kerchief and lay it in his mother's hands: "Here, Mother, Virtus' mother, Julia, sent this for you."

Ina exclaimed: "Oh, a lovely, white handkerchief! How beautiful it is!"

Geron said: "There is something inside." Ina unfolded the linen cloth and there was the gold necklace. She was overcome by its beauty. Geron said: "It's a necklace for you, Mother, from Julia, for all the worry I have caused you." Ina held the necklace to her throat and Geron fastened it for her.

It seemed very strange to Ina that she should have something that beautiful for herself. She said: "I will wear it on festival days. But it is too special to wear while milking the cows or doing the house-work. Today is a festive day since you are back, my dear Geron, and I will wear it today!"

Gerda said: "You should also wear it while spinning, singing, and for story time, Mother. It is nice for the eyes to look at gold!"

Geron asked: "Father, what was Wugo's burial like?"

His father reported: "When they knew he was dying, Evart, the Druid, came to his bedside. He helped him through it. Then Evart directed that on the third day they should bury him by the big rock at the edge of the forest. They wrapped his body in the bear skin that he lay on while he was ill. I helped to bury him. We lay his weapons beside him in the grave. Evart spoke a few words which were something like: 'The body goes into the Earth and the soul returns to its home.' Runege was very upset so Evart asked Helga to move in with her for a while and help her since Runege was not capable of running the house and farm. Evart also asked Helga to sing for Runege so her spirit could find comfort in the music. Helga's parents agreed to let her stay. So, the girl is now looking after Runege as well as the old servants, Bur and Bor."

Geron said: "I will give the Roman silver to Runege and I will work for her as well if Bur and Bor cannot handle everything. I owe it to Wugo."

Geron reached further into his leather pouch and pulled out the bronze lamp with the horse's head decoration. He did not tell them what it was. It went from hand to hand and everyone admired the likeness of the horse. Geron brought out the well-sealed oil bottle, filled the lamp, and lit it with a stick from the fire. The oil lamp was once again passed around for all to see how the horse's head was now illumined.

Gerwin asked: "Will it burn now day and night, the whole year?"

Geron replied: "The lamp uses up the oil as it burns. When no more oil is inside then the lamp goes out. That is why we have to conserve the oil. But it will bring us much happiness on many long, winter evenings."

Uralda said: "There is oil in walnuts. When the Roman oil is used up I will press the walnuts and make German oil." Everyone laughed at the time, but later Uralda did exactly that.

Ina suggested: "Since Wugo's burial we have not paid much attention to poor Runege. Wugo's farm is our nearest neighbor. We can visit Runege this afternoon. Geron can bring her the reward money."

But German said: "You all can go. I am going to make some posts with the new ax. The sheep pen should be improved."

And Uralda said: "I am not going to sit upon a horse. I would rather stay here where it is warm and spin my wool."

The Ride to Wugo's Farm

The thaw had begun. The fields were free of snow by midday. Geron let Gerda and Gerwin go for a trial ride on Fire Fox. Fire Fox allowed himself to be handled easily with a bit in his mouth and reins. Geron decided it would be safe to let his younger siblings ride on Fire Fox to Wugo's farm. Ina rode German's horse. So, in the early afternoon three horses left German's farm.

When they were close to Wugo's farm, Geron said: "I am going to ride ahead a little to make sure the dogs will not bother us." He galloped off. There was no barking to be heard when he reached the house. Bur and Bor had taken both dogs with them to the sheep stable. Geron tied his horse to the fencepost just like he had always done. He walked to the house.

But what was that he heard? It was singing! Geron slowly crept toward the door. Helga was singing the song about the water fairy who missed the shepherd who watched over the sheep by the water. And so, she had pulled him into the deep water. Yes, Geron recognized this song. Helga had sung it that time he was hiding in the bushes and listening. From that time on he had been in love with Helga's singing voice. He stepped quietly onto the threshold. Helga began a different song. Geron pulled aside the animal skin over the door. He forgot that the light streaming in from outside would alert the women to his presence. The singing suddenly stopped. Helga gave a startled cry: "Geron!" She hurried to the door. He walked in. She gave him a big hug as if he were her brother. She said: "Geron, you're back? You aren't hurt?!" Tears were streaming down her face.

Geron had not expected such a greeting from Helga. She took his hand and led him to Runege and said: "Look, Runege, Geron is back!"

Runege, who had not been herself since Wugo's death, looked up and said: "Took the Roman away! Took the Roman away; that's bad. Wugo very angry!"

Voices from outside could be heard. Ina and her other two children were standing in the doorway. Helga invited them inside and Ina went to Runege's side. She was ill and lying on sheepskin rugs. She hardly knew the guests. Geron tossed some tree bark onto the fire to give more light. Ina and the children sat to talk to Runege. She was able to remember only Ina's name. Geron tried to explain to Helga in a few words about his stay with the Romans and how happy Virtus was.

Gerwin called: "The dogs are coming!" Geron and Helga quickly went outside with the children. Helga had befriended the dogs. They happily barked their greetings. They left the horses alone and drove the sheep into their pen. Bur and Bor were cleaner than before and dressed in a more orderly fashion. Geron thought that must have been Helga's doing. She had brought the good habits of the Holding household into Wugo's home.

Now Bur and Bor wanted to hear what Geron had to tell about his adventure with the slave, Virtus. Helga said: "Come over here by the fire. There is enough oatmeal for everyone." While they were sitting around the fire, the dogs could be heard barking once again.

Geron went outside to see what the matter was. A white horse could be seen coming toward the house. Sitting upon the horse were Evart and Holger! Geron hurried to meet them at the gate. Holger cried: "Geron!" He jumped from the horse and ran to his friend.

Evart stopped the horse and looked lovingly at the two friends. Geron and Holger approached Evart. Evart dismounted. Geron could not find any words. Was Evart angry with him? Just as he had done before, Evart put both hands on Geron's shoulders and looked intently into his eyes. His face lightened. He said, almost cheerfully: "The Roman wolf did not bite you!" Geron understood what he meant. The Druid gave Geron a fatherly hug and said to him: "It will be a blessing for many that you have returned to your homeland so quickly, Geron. You have become a man!"

Inside once again, Geron told the story of his adventure with Virtus and the Romans. There was only one person not listening. Runege had fallen asleep. Once, while Geron was telling about the stone gods of the Romans, Runege woke up and asked Helga to sing to her. Helga looked at Evart and he said: "Yes, Helga, sing!" She sang a song about the wind, the oldest wanderer upon the Earth and how Odhin travels throughout the world on the wind. When she was finished Runege had already fallen asleep again. Geron told about the boat ride on the Rhine River.

It was time to do the evening chores. Wugo's farm held about ten cows and steers. Geron and the children offered to help Bur and Bor. Evart went for a walk with Ina around the farm. They talked about the future of Runege and her farm. Everyone came in and gathered around once again for some evening repast of milk and bread.

Evart spoke: "Runege's Norns have gathered us all here this evening. I have read the signs for her. It is too much for Helga to take on the heavy burden of Wugo's farm and the old folks alone. Ina has said she is prepared to stay here over the winter with Helga and help her take care of the household. She will speak with German about it and if he agrees, she will return tomorrow with Geron. Geron can be a help to Bur and Bor. At the next Druid Gathering in the spring Geron must step into the ring and explain himself to the judge and council of the elders as to why he helped Virtus escape. Do not worry, Geron! You did a brave deed and you can make restitution now by helping Runege with the farm."

Geron asked: "Father Evart, what should I do with the silver money that I brought for Wugo?"

The Druid answered: "The council of elders will decide at the Gathering. Until then, keep it safe. The mice certainly won't eat it!"

The Winter Solstice

Deep snow lay over the forest. Soon the shortest day of the year would be upon them. Residents from all over began gathering at the Holy Site to celebrate the winter solstice. German's family and Holding's family had come on horseback. Holger had been staying with the Druids for a few days already and helping them with the preparations for the festival. There was a large pile of wood ready to be lit. A big elk was to be sacrificed. It had been captured alive. Everyone who came brought gifts for the Druids: cheese, butter, eggs, meat, and grain. The fire would be lit at nightfall.

When Geron arrived with his family, Holger walked up to him and greeted him: "The old sun dies and a new one is born! Health and happiness be with you!"

Holger took these words of greeting to one person after the other. When he reached his mother, Hulda, she hugged him and said: "In the new year of the Sun you will be fourteen years old and will go to live with the Druids forever!" In spite of the pain of letting her son go, Hulda was very proud of him for being chosen to follow in the wise path of the Druids.

Holger greeted his brother Hoegge, who asked him: "What's to eat?"

Holger answered: "An elk will be sacrificed – a sun animal. His antlers will be given to the one who draws the shortest stick."

Hoegge remarked: "I don't want the antlers. But if I can get some meat from the leg, I can surely run faster!"

The visitors at the Sun Festival had all brought containers in which to put some coals from the sacrificial fire to take home with them. For as soon as dawn of the shortest day of the year arrived, all the fires in German homes must be put out in order to begin a new year with a new, blessed fire in the hearth. Runege, Bur, and Bor sat in the dark at Wugo's farm waiting for the others to return with the coals for their new fire. Uralda sat in the dark in German's house and Grandfather Helge was doing the same at the Holdings' farm. Everyone was anxiously awaiting the return of the celebrants.

It was a night bright with starlight. A row of singing priests could be seen and heard coming from the Druid farm. They carried burning torches. The waiting people became silent. As the priests got closer one could understand the words they were singing:

The Old Sun dies,
A New Sun is born.
So did Baldur die,
And will be born again!

Hoegge whispered to Geron: "Baldur was the one who was shot with the arrow, wasn't he? Did I not say that one should bring him back again?" Geron gave Hoegge a dried pear so that he would have something to chew on during the ceremony.

Twelve Druids came. Behind them were the student helpers leading the elk for the sacrifice. The Druids formed a circle around the wood for the fire and when they gave the sign the fire was lit. The high priest spoke a few words, the other priests repeated what he said, and then the onlookers repeated. Some of the Druids tossed special herbs into the flames and others threw in some pine resin. The flames were so hot that the people had to back up a little so there was a wide space between them and the fire. They all began to walk in one direction around the fire. It looked like a moving wheel of people.

One Druid gave a sign for them to stop. He asked: "Are there any young people present who would like to declare their engagement for the coming new year?" Two couples came out of the crowd, hand in hand, and began to dance and jump in front of the fire. One of the couples was Geron and Helga. Hoegge, who had not been listening closely to what the priest said, heard only the last few words, something about jumping around the fire. He quickly jumped into the light and gave his best effort at a wild dance around the flames. Everyone laughed.

For the German people the Sun Fire was the place where one openly declared one's intention to be married in the coming year. So, after the dancing ended the couples were congratulated by one and all. Naturally, Geron's and Helga's parents gave their kind congratulations.

A wooden hammer was struck three times on a wooden plank. Everyone was silent once again. The sacrifice began. The elk head with the antlers was put on a pole by the fire. At a signal from the high priest the animal was butchered and pieces of meat were put on spits to roast. The people sat upon animal skins that they had brought with them. Jugs of mead were handed around to drink. Soon the call was made for the heads of all the families to come get some meat from the spits. They put the meat in the containers that would later contain the coals from the fire.

The families of German and Holding were all in a festive mood. When Hoegge was asked who his bride was who did not show up at the fire dance, he answered: "She ran away from me!"

Evart mingled with the guests and greeted family after family. When he came to the Germans and the Holdings, he had a gentle smile on his face and said: "The Norns whispered to me that you would take the dance around the fire today. Helga, remain true to your singing. Geron, build a new house!"

Slowly the families began to fill their clay containers with coals. They covered the coals with ashes to keep them hot on the long trip home. The new fires should be lit around midnight.

Before the two families parted, Holger spoke to Geron so that only he could hear: "Evart told me that the Druids will now go into a cave for the night. With their spiritual eyes they can see the Sun at midnight as it shines on the other side of the world. They stay up the whole night in prayer to ask for the gods' blessings for the new year. In the spring I will be taken in by them as a student and live with them always. But, Geron, our friendship will never die!"

The Druid Gathering

Spring arrived. Runege had been buried at Wugo's farm. Since she had no children or close relatives, it would be decided at the next Druid Gathering what was to become of the farm. The day when the nights and days were of equal length was the day devoted to the Druid Gathering.

After Runege's death, Helga had gone back to her family and Ina returned to hers. Geron had to stay alone with Bur and Bor and look after the farm. The fields had to be prepared for spring planting. According to custom, Geron and Helga would be married a little later in the year after the Gathering. Geron was a little worried that the elders might punish him for kidnapping Virtus. His father had advised him to ask Evart to be there. Geron had asked him at the Winter Solstice Festival. Evart said: "I will be there and speak for you. You must speak the truth, openly and without fear!" That was why Geron had confidence that everything would work out for the best.

Those going to the Gathering started out early in the morning from all directions in a wide area. There was an immense linden tree standing in the middle of the meadow reserved for the Gathering. There were rocks arranged around the linden tree that served as stools for the elders of the council and the judge. There were posts stuck in a circle around the tree, a little wider than the crown of the tree. A rope was strung between the posts. This was known as the "Ring." The judge and the elders sat inside the ring under the linden tree. Plaintiffs and defendants had to step into the ring. The people had to stand outside the ring and listen to the proceedings.

There was a large judgment sword leaning against the tree. The executioner sat next to the sword. Last year he had to cut off the head of an arsonist. Another man had three fingers of his right hand cut off because he would not stop stealing. Not far from the linden tree stood the "Dead Man's Tree" with its dry, dead branches. Two years ago the executioner had hung a horse thief on that tree and the ravens ate his flesh after he was dead.

The crowd was waiting around the ring. They heard the horn blowing. Three Druids and the elders were walking from the Druid farm. Evart was among them. The "Ring" was opened for them to enter and then closed behind them. With great ceremony the Druids took their seats. The speaker for the elders raised his voice: "The Gathering has now begun! Here in the ring shall truth and right hold sway! Whoever is called into the ring steps before the eye of Truth, the eye of Divinity, which sees that which is hidden. The names of those who will appear in the ring at this Gathering have been made known. Call the first name!"

The Druid, Waro, stood and called: "Sigvart, Hunding's son, shall step forward!" A young man ducked under the rope into the ring.

The elder spoke: "You are charged with taking a sheep from the herd of your neighbor, Ingo, when his herd was grazing close to your field. What say you?"

The young man answered in a repressed voice: "I did it in a dark moment. I am sorry for it and ask for forgiveness. I will give Ingo three sheep in return."

The elders and the Druids deliberated among themselves for a little while. Waro stepped forward and said: "Your regret and your repayment have been accepted. Bow down before the Sword of Judgment." The executioner took the sword and lay the flat side on Sigvart's bowed head. Ingo now stepped into the ring with Sigvart, his neighbor. They gave each other the handshake of forgiveness. Everything was settled and they left the ring.

Waro called out the next name: "Gunther, son of Hilpert, step into the ring! The elder said: "You are charged with stealing meat gotten from a hunt with Herman. You quickly butchered the animal when Herman went off to borrow a horse to transport the kill back home. What say you?"

Gunther was very nervous: "I thought Herman had forgotten to take the animal and so I thought I would take it home and butcher it before the meat went bad. I gave him the skin, the meat, and the innards of the elk."

The judge said: "You did that only after Herman came to your house and found everything there. Before he came inside your house you pretended to know nothing of the elk." The elders and the Druids deliberated once again.

Waro stepped forward: "You have shown no remorse. You tried to get out of it by telling lies. As punishment, you will have two fingers chopped off your right hand. Put your hand on the block!" There was nothing more that could be said. The executioner cut off the two outer fingers of his right hand. Gunther screamed and disappeared from the meadow.

The elder said: "Hunding, the son of Walo, step into the ring!" Hunding did so. The elder said: "Hunding, a Druid has made a complaint against you. You have six children at home, the youngest but a babe. Last spring you left your family on your horse. You had adventures in the world. Your wife and children had to do all the work at home during the entire summer. Neighbors came to their aid in your place. You returned in autumn after all the harvest and field work was finished. And you sat around the warm fire and ate the winter provisions. You left your family for a half-year. What say you?"

Hunding stared at the ground and stuttered out a few words, then he was silent.

Waro stepped forward and said: "At this Gathering you shall get a lesson that you will not soon forget. Executioner, put this man in the stocks and stick him in the swamp until this evening!" The executioner took a two-part contraption and put it around Hunding's neck in such a way that he would not sink completely into the quicksand.

A few people went along to watch. One of them said: "It takes a long time for a man to look clean in another's eyes when he has been sunk in the swamp. Poor man!"

The Druid called out the last name: "Geron, son of German, step into the ring!" Even though Geron felt like his blood was curdling, he stepped bravely into the ring. The elder spoke: "Wugo, who has since died, made a complaint against you months ago. You helped his slave escape back to Roman territory. Justice continues even after death. What say you?"

Geron began: "Honorable Fathers! I remain indebted to Wugo who has departed this life. I admit it! My heart was moved by the suffering and homesickness of the Roman slave. Freedom is the highest good for the Romans as well as for us. I wanted to bring Wugo ransom money when I returned. I carry here in my leather pouch silver money, enough to buy five cows. Wugo told me the slave was worth three cows. Since my return I have worked the entire winter for Wugo's widow, Runege. Since she died, I have been taking care of the farm with the two servants, Bur and Bor."

When Geron had finished Sigmann stepped into the ring with his son, Sigbert, to be witnesses for Geron. The Druid allowed him to speak. He said: "Fathers, look upon my son, Sigbert. He was but a boy when the Romans captured him and put him up for sale at a Roman slave market. He would still be there if not for Geron. Geron used his influence and was able to secure my son's freedom. He even offered his own horse as payment. He brought back our dear son to us. Because of Geron our lives are no longer burdened by sadness. We will be grateful to him forever!"

The council of elders and the Druids deliberated a long time. Sigmann and Sigbert remained with Geron inside the ring. Finally Waro stepped forward and said: "We are not friends of the power of the Roman Wolf, but even among Romans there are people who exhibit great gratitude. Such people have given you the silver, Geron. They have further helped you to secure freedom for Sigbert. You shall turn over the silver to the council of elders to be used as needed for those requiring assistance. Your noble act in the case of Sigbert has served to relieve you of all guilt."

The onlookers could be heard murmuring their approval and many swords could be heard clattering against shields as a kind of applause. Evart stepped forward and raised his voice: "Germans and those of the Druid Gathering! I helped Wugo and Runege enter into the realm of the dead. Their Norns are satisfied if Geron will continue to take care of the farm. Is there anyone present who has the right of inheritance?" Nobody stepped forward to claim that right. Evart continued: "Then what the elders have decided will remain in effect: Geron shall become master of Wugo's farm!"

Geron took the silver that Julus Severus had given him and turned it over to the council of elders. Sigbert took Geron's hand and asked: "May I come and help on the farm?"

Geron replied: "Yes, Sigbert, you may. Come today! I am grateful for your help." The two left the ring. Geron whispered to Sigbert: "Come on, let's jump over the rope!" Geron received good wishes from all sides. But Helga was the one who was happiest at the outcome and her tears turned to tears of joy.

The elders and the Druids stood. They sang a song in praise of justice. The ring was opened and they left the Gathering to return to the farm.

Holding spoke: "Let's all go back to our farm. It's the closest. We must celebrate this wonderful day!" Helga had ridden Fire Fox to the Gathering. She sat behind Geron on his horse so that Sigbert could ride Fire Fox. Sigbert was very pleased. Soon they were on their way to Holding's house. The best smoked meat was taken down from the rafters and a festive meal was prepared.

Hoegge, Gerwin, and Gerda had stayed at Holding's farm. Grandfather Helge had kept Gerda busy churning butter. The boys had milked the cows and goats. So now the children could also enjoy the celebration. There was eating, drinking, singing, and games. Holding told his jokes, and laughter was heard late into the night.

It was long past midnight when Geron and Sigbert got back to Wugo's farm. Bur and Bor were asleep in the straw. Geron had trained the dogs to stop barking when he called them. He greeted them with kind words and threw them some bones to gnaw.

Geron led Sigbert into the dark house to the fire so he would not stumble. He lit his little oil lamp. They both sat by the warm hearth. They spoke of the city of Castra Vetera, of Virtus, Claudia, the villa of Julus Severus, and the temples of the Roman gods and goddesses. Suddenly Sigbert asked: "Geron, do you still have that magic wax tablet? I have often thought of it."

Geron answered: "Yes, I wrapped it in leather and put it away carefully. Virtus told me that what was written on it would always give me safe passage through Roman territory. I can visit him whenever I want. Maybe I will go with Helga for a visit sometime this year and my Roman friends will become her friends as well."

Sigbert asked: "And what about your new house?"

Geron answered: "After the spring grain crop has been seeded, Holding will come and help us begin building a new house. Then, Sigbert, there will be much work for us and the horses."

Sigbert agreed: "Yes, I can't wait! And we will go hunting together and get a nice elk so that the new house can have sun antlers displayed on the wall."